The Feminine Sixth:
WOMEN
for
the
DEFENSE

By Andrea D. Lyon

For Customer Service, Call 1-202-465-7661

Cover Design: Cathy Zlomek

The Feminine Sixth: Women for the Defense

Feminine

1. female 1a(1)

2. characteristic of or appropriate or unique to women; *feminine beauty*; *a feminine perspective*

3. of, relating to, or constituting the gender that ordinarily includes most words or grammatical forms referring to females; *a feminine noun**

Amendment VI

In all criminal prosecutions, the accused shall enjoy the right to a speedy and public trial, by an impartial jury of the State and district wherein the crime shall have been committed, which district shall have been previously ascertained by law, and to be informed of the nature and cause of the accusation; to be confronted with the witnesses against him; to have compulsory process for obtaining witnesses in his favor, and to have the Assistance of Counsel for his defence.

Sixth Sense

If you say that someone has a sixth sense, you mean that they seem to have a natural ability to know about things before other people, or to know things that other people do not know.**

* https://www.merriam-webster.com/dictionary/feminine
** https://www.collinsdictionary.com/us/dictionary/english/sixth-sense

To the fabulous women who were so kind as to share their stories with me for this book, to my other sisters-in-arms who fight the good fight, and for my actual sisters, Rachel and Erica, and my brother Jon.

ACKNOWLEDGEMENTS

There are many people to thank, but first and foremost I want to thank the National Association of Criminal Defense Lawyers for hosting the program that led to this book, a discussion of women in criminal defense where Lisa Wayne interviewed me and the idea was born. I want to thank NACDL's executive director, Norman Reimer and most importantly, Ivan Dominguez for his support, spirit, and great editing. I also thank Valparaiso University where I have the privilege to work, its President Dr. Mark A. Heckler, and Provost Dr. Mark L. Biermann for their support. My two assistants Linda Nelson and then Laurie Beach were invaluable, as was court reporter Carmen Fagan who transcribed the many hours of interviews. I also want to thank Randi McGinn and Charlie Daniels who gave me house room to write in when I needed it, not to mention love and encouragement.

TABLE OF CONTENTS

FOREWORD

By Emily Hughes*

Andrea Lyon is a trial attorney to the bone. The beauty of this book is that because a trial attorney wrote it, the words lift off the page as if Andrea is talking with you. Somehow, somewhere, Andrea got the idea to interview nine female criminal defense attorneys and learn what they have in common and where their lives diverge. Then she traveled across the country, from coast to coast, interviewing women she knew and women she didn't know. The young lawyers and seasoned veterans she found span a spectrum of diversity, from geography to religion to race; some married, some single, some divorced; with children, without children; public defenders and private attorneys, including one woman who has left criminal defense to pursue other work. The beauty of this book is that because a trial attorney wrote it, not only Andrea's voice but the voices of each woman resonate as if we are sitting in a room talking together.

In true trial attorney fashion, Andrea left no stone unturned while she found her witnesses: nine women who were willing to share their personal stories and in so doing, effectively testify to deeply private choices and forces that helped shape their lives. From empathy and emotion in their work to confronting moral repugnance and work/life balance, these subjects speak to each of our identities and help us better understand the

---

* Emily Hughes is a criminal defense attorney and the Associate Dean for Faculty and Academic Affairs and Professor and Bouma Fellow in Law at the University of Iowa College of Law, recipient of a Harvard fellowship, and a former student of Andrea Lyon's.

The Feminine Sixth: Women for the Defense

choices we've made in our own lives. The fact that the nine women interviewed for this book shared what they did is a testament to their selflessness, and it is also a testament to trusting what Andrea would do with their stories.

Understanding the nine lives interwoven through this book is the first step to understanding how each woman — individually and collectively — is the tip of the iceberg of incredible people who defend those charged with crimes. This book is a point in time that captures a precise moment in nine different lives. Each woman reflects on what she does and why she does it while also discussing what has come before and what is to come. The book is filled with laughter and longing and hope. It is familiar while also being tangibly alive. It packs a punch in the most surprising of moments, all the while holding the reader safe through the journey.

The questions and follow-up questions show Andrea hearing what her interviewees are saying while also understanding what they are not saying. She follows the trail of their spoken words while also digging deeply into the space between their words to hear what would have otherwise remained unsaid. Part of the joy of this book is to see Andrea's mind move at the same time we see her interviewees' minds move. The reader watches Andrea's thought process while also peeking into the minds of nine truly amazing female criminal defense attorneys. They each tell their own stories, and together their individual stories form a single thread.

This book is not a powerful narrative because the women's individual lives are so interesting — although they certainly are. Rather, this book is powerful because each woman's story resonates and rises beyond their individual lives and their chosen profession. Their stories touch core issues that reach us all, no matter what race, age, gender, socio-economic class, sexual orientation, or profession.

Law students and lawyers will see themselves and learn more about themselves through this book, even if they have no interest in criminal defense, and even if they are not a woman. Indeed, people may learn more about themselves by reading this book especially if they are not a woman, for this book brings the reader into a deeply personal conversation that people who live in this space — let alone people outside of this space — rarely see.

But maybe one would expect all this from a book about lawyers. One might expect the book to speak to lawyers and law students and transcend gender by pulling in readers who are not exactly like any of the women in the book.

At the same time, perhaps you are skeptical that this book could reach beyond the law and speak to people who aren't lawyers or who don't want to become lawyers. I have to admit that I shared that concern at first. When Andrea told me about this project, I knew I would learn something important by hearing the stories she told. But I'm a criminal defense attorney, so that's kind of a given. I was somewhat skeptical that the book would be interesting — let alone captivating — to people who aren't lawyers.

When I sat down to read the book, I looked forward to being swept into a world I knew — a world that is my own world, a world where I know some of the people she interviewed.

What I was not prepared for was how much I didn't know about the people I thought I knew. What I was not prepared for was how much the book would make me think about my own choices, my own dreams, and my own life path. What

The Feminine Sixth: Women for the Defense

I was not prepared for was how much the book would be about so much more than the lives of the nine women in it.

I finished the book in one sitting. One glorious, luscious, fall-into-the-pages-and-don't-put-it-down read. When I turned the last page, two distinct impressions stuck in my mind.

The first was that it was startling that the conversation in this book never happened. The "conceit," as Andrea describes it, is that she is hosting a symposium and the nine women she interviewed are at the symposium together, talking to one other and spontaneously responding to Andrea's questions. In reality, Andrea interviewed each woman individually, one-on-one in hotel rooms, restaurants, and offices across the country. Then she transcribed each interview and wove each individual response into the shared narrative. Andrea's individual conversations with each woman really happened, but none of the women talked to each other or heard what each other said. Nobody was ever in the same room together, except for Andrea and the person she was interviewing. Because the seam of the book is so tightly constructed, it is easy to imagine the nine women in the same room together, and it is striking that they weren't.

Which brings me to the second impression I had when I finished the book: these nine women need to be in the same room together. There has to be an opportunity for people to read the book, then attend a symposium to hear these nine women talk about their lives as portrayed through the book. There has to be an opportunity for the next chapter — the chapter in which the women reflect about the process of being interviewed, then the process of picking up the book and reading their own words: words they really said, now woven into a fictional dialogue that never happened. There has to be an opportunity to hear again from the women in this book, to learn what they themselves learned through the process. To hear their questions for one another. To hear our questions for them. In short, the symposium that forms the conceit of this book should happen.

As this book goes to press, much is right and much is falling apart in the world around us. This book will make you think. Read it and pass it along. Give it to your niece or nephew or neighbor. Give it your client or colleague.

Share this book with somebody you care about because we need more frank conversations like those captured in this book in order to understand ourselves and our neighbors. We need more frank conversations like the conversation in this book because we need to listen to one another just a little better. To understand one another just a little more. And in the spirit of listening to the stories that Andrea and her interviewees so bravely tell us, perhaps we could all benefit from being just a little more brave.

INTRODUCTION

I had been trying to find him for months. I didn't know much about where to look, and this was before the days of online searching (in the mid-1980s), so the only thing for it was old-fashioned shoe leather. I needed him though. He had been attacked, shot, and left for dead by the deceased in a murder case I was preparing for, a case where we were alleging self-defense.

The wrinkle was that my client was a woman, the deceased was a woman, and they were roommates. Okay, more than roommates. And, believe me, being gay was enough to get you convicted all by itself back then. I knew my client's statements about her belief her lover would kill her if she didn't get to the gun first would not be enough. I needed to be able to prove the deceased was actually deadly.

Here was the problem. My client knew the previous victim's street name — Abdullah — and not much else. She knew he was a pool player, that this was how he made his money, and that he was a south-sider, that he was also African American (as was she and the deceased), and the names of three pool halls he might have gone to. He was about 5 feet 10 inches in height, medium complexioned, and average weight. Great. That was going to describe just about everyone.

I tried asking folks in the neighborhood where my client had lived. I asked former clients, and their relatives. I went to all three pool halls and asked their managers. All three claimed

The Feminine Sixth: Women for the Defense

not to know the guy. But one of them, well I just felt he did know, he just wasn't going to tell some white woman from the public defenders' office. I certainly noticed that there were NO women in any of the pool halls, let alone anyone white.

So, when it became clear we were going to trial with or without this mysterious Abdullah, I decided to try the pool hall on 63rd and Langley where I had that inkling from the manager. This time though, I stationed myself outside the pool hall on public sidewalk and stopped everyone going in or out of the place for a couple of hours. The third night I did this, the manager came out.

"Girl, you know you bad for business," he said. I hadn't ever seen someone harrumph before, but he harrumphed.

I smiled. "Well I need to find Abdullah, and I don't know how else to do it," I replied. I shrugged, "Someone is going to know him, sooner or later I figure." I turned away from him to face another young man who was coming towards the door of the pool hall but he saw me and turned away.

I heard the manager muttering as he went back into the pool hall. Half an hour later, Abdullah was there. And he had a harrowing story to tell, and the records to back it up.

I believe I found this witness because I am a woman. It's not that men don't persevere; they do. It's not that they aren't willing to spend lots of time trying to solve a problem by regular means and, failing that, will try something else. They will.

It's that I knew I was looked at askance anyway. As a woman defending murder cases and death penalty cases, I didn't belong. So not belonging was a norm for me, and I was willing to (rather loudly) not belong for my client.

This book tells the stories of some extraordinary women that you likely do not know. They have all been or are still criminal defense lawyers. They have all had differing experiences doing this work, figuring out how to live their lives while doing it, and being aware of how their gender affected or still affects those choices and styles. The book comes from lengthy in person interviews with nine extraordinary women, whom you will meet shortly. The "conceit" is that we are all presenting a panel on the work we do for Women's History Month. I have edited each of the women's statements to make grammar work, or transitions sensible, but these are our words and our stories.

The Sixth Amendment guarantees those charged with crimes the right to effective assistance of counsel. The only lawyers recognized by the Constitution are us. These are the stories of that part of that constitutional mandate that are women (a relatively new occurrence); the feminine Sixth.

CHAPTER ONE:
HOW DID SHE GET HERE?

I look out into the crowded auditorium. There are students and faculty from all over the university it seems, lots of talking and looking around. I check (again) to be sure the long table for the panel has water, enough microphones, name placards, and pads and pens for taking notes. We have a nice set up — the panelists will be on large screens on either side of the stage simultaneously with the presentation.

This is a very unusual Women's History Month presentation; every one of the ten of us (including me) are or were criminal defense lawyers. We are women representing the "bad guys" of the system, those who are despised, and many of whom wouldn't have dreamed of hiring us to defend them. I smile to myself at that thought, I certainly remember those days; as the first woman to be lead counsel defending someone facing the death penalty, I faced a lot of doubters.

I am so happy with who we have coming to speak, and the fact that they have agreed to discuss so many issues of interest — personal and professional — with everyone. These nine panelists include women at the beginning of their careers, some in the middle, and some closer to or at the end of their careers. Some of them I knew before inviting them to participate, some I didn't. They are black, white, and Latina. They are Christian, atheist, Jewish, and Muslim. They are from the eastern, western, midwestern, and southern parts of our country. They are public defenders and private

The Feminine Sixth: Women for the Defense

practitioners and some who have been both. And they have such interesting stories to tell.

I debate whether to introduce them all at once, but decide against it. It will make more sense if the introduction is tied to their first presentation. I look at my watch, it's almost time. So I go back to the 'green room' where everyone is and let them know we are going to start in a few minutes. The atmosphere in the room is a combination of nervousness and hilarity.

We go out onto the stage, there are two podiums, one for me on stage right and one for the panelists (if they prefer to stand) on stage left. There is a long table in the middle with a white tablecloth.

I walk out, followed by the panelists who take their seats. The lights flash a few times, and people start to take their seats. I ask them to be seated, and slowly the conversation dies down and their attention is on me.

Photo Credit: Dorothy Freedman

"Welcome everyone to this year's Women's History Month event. My name is **Andrea Lyon,** and I will be moderating our panel of women criminal defense lawyers. I am also a defense lawyer, and have been for a long time in one form or another. I just want to take a minute to explain the program; this is organized by topic, so we will start with introductions and each of these women's path to becoming a criminal defense lawyer. Then, we will cover the next two parts of the program, which are emotions in our work and being a woman in a white man's world. We will then break for lunch, and cover the remaining topics this afternoon. They are: confronting moral repugnance, life/work balance, fighting as feminine, and then a wrap up. After each panelist has spoken on each topic, I will invite questions, but not too many, okay? We have a lot of ground to cover." I take a breath. "One other matter. The nature of criminal defense is contrarian and not particularly politically correct, so some of the language may be a bit salty, and, well, we joke about things others might not. It's hard to explain to normal people that you tell autopsy jokes." There is some laughter in the audience, so that makes me feel a bit better. "So let me start by introducing our first panelist — I am going in alphabetical order by last name for lack of any better way to figure it out."

"**Juanita Brooks** is probably best known in criminal defense circles for her successful defense of John DeLorean. She was a member of the highly regarded San Diego Federal Defender's Office, and then in private practice as a criminal defense lawyer. She left criminal defense and is now a Principal of the firm Fish Richardson, and an elected member of the firm's Management Committee. She is a nationally recognized trial and appellate lawyer who specializes in complex intellectual property, product liability, and mass tort litigation. In 2014, she was named 'Litigator of the Year' by The American Lawyer. Ms. Brooks, called "a titan of the patent bar," has been lead counsel in more than 13 patent trials over the past two years, and has handled more than 150 trials in her career. Please help me welcome Juanita Brooks!" There is applause and Juanita walks to the podium.

"Good morning, everyone. When Andrea asked me to do this, I asked he if she was sure — I felt like a poser since I don't do criminal defense anymore, but she talked me into it. Have you ever tried to say no to Andrea Lyon?" She asks the

The Feminine Sixth: Women for the Defense

other panelists. There is a lot of head shaking and laughter. "I am Mexican, or at least part Mexican. I was born in Merced, California in 1954, on the Air Force base, Castle Air Force Base, because at that point my father was in the Air Force. And my mother — my father was my mother's third husband. My mother had come from Belgium where she had lived. She was ten years older than my dad, and she had lived through the war in occupied Belgium. I had a half-sister, who was the product of my mother's second marriage, who was six years older than me. My memories of my father from when I was little were that he was very Hispanic, we would have serapes in our house and the bullhorns on the wall, and he would play Spanish music, and he was very sweet and loving. He was 23 when I was born, so that's like a baby. But he was just a very sweet, loving man who loved to have a good time, loved to drink. And my recollection is that my mother hated him, and so she had married him because she was desperate. Her second husband, the one who brought her to the U.S., had left her. So she was a decade older than my father and didn't like anything about his — the fact that he was Mexican, didn't like the serapes, didn't like the music, didn't like the food, and was always critical of that. And my mother, in those days, you would refer to someone like her as high strung." Juanita uses air quotes for those last two words.

"My dad got transferred to Minong, North Dakota, a very desolate spot. It makes Fargo look like a garden city. It was just brutal there, the winters were brutal. There was nothing to do. So my sister, at the age of 14, got herself knocked up, and my dad could not handle it, just absolutely could not handle it. So he then got transferred to the Philippines, and rather than take us all with him, he dropped us off in California on his way out of town and just never came back. So he left my mother, my sister, her 16-year-old boyfriend, and me, outside of an Air Force base so we could use the commissary and stuff like that, but in Sunnymead, California, and he was gone.

And it's way too painful and hard for me to talk about what that felt like. We had no money and so we — and my mother had a breakdown, and my sister was a 15-year-old mother. So I sort of became the matriarch."

"We took in laundry, which I did. We did an illegal day care, and there I am, ten years old, watching the other kids. And what we did basically is whatever we had to do to try to make ends meet. So those were really grim — that was a really grim time. You know, we lived in a really bad neighborhood and not a lot of happy memories from that time period." Juanita pauses, and takes a breath. "The fact that I am a lawyer, that I am anything, is kind of an accidental miracle. School was an escape, so school was where I was happy. School was where I could get out of the dysfunctionality of my home. So it did come, I think, very easy for me because it was something that I loved and could excel at and they would have a hard time taking away."

"I had this good friend in high school Mary Ellen and she was so excited about going to State, and so I said, 'Oh, well, I'll go, too.' So I ended up going to San Diego State with Mary Ellen and that's how I ended up in college. But for that — and my mother was furious with me. She wanted me to stay home and take care of her and work at the 7-Eleven like all the other kids were doing. Why did I have to go away, 'away,' meaning it was an hour drive down San Diego, but why did I have to do that? And she was very much opposed to it. It was a four-year school that I did in three. It wasn't a junior college, it was a university, but I had to get myself through it so I just sat down with a course book and figured out how many units I would have to take every semester and how many over the summer in order do it in three years, and just sat down, planned. Plus I was working. I had to work obviously to pay. So it was 20 units a semester and six units in the summer, and then I could get through in three years. So that's what I did. It wasn't a real college experience. It was pretty much just put my head down and keep going."

I look at the other panelists. There is such pain and longing in Juanita's voice, they see it, hear it, and identify with it. I am thinking how eerily similar Juanita's story and mine are — not the part about being poor, I never was that, but my mother broke down when I was 10, and I had to grow up fast too. And I finished college in three years, I was in such a hurry.

Juanita continues, "law school is another story of 'but for.' One of my classes was Model United Nations, and it was run by this professor, Professor Generales, and he was looking for an assistant, a TA. I picked Ecuador as my country and immediately declared that my fishing waters were 500 miles or something, 300 miles, and if any other country came into my fishing waters, I would seize their ships. (Laughter.) It was, like, 'You're freaking Ecuador, for God's sake. You can't do this kind of stuff.' 'Of course I can. I can do anything I want. This is the MUN.' So Professor Generales spotted me and thought, okay, that girl's got potential. So he asked me to be his TA, so obviously that was one job. Then he also was involved in the International Council on World Affairs, and they needed a secretary, so I got another job. And they were both thankfully — so he really kind of became my mentor. And he said, 'Well, what are you going to do after college?' And I say, 'I haven't really thought about it.' He said, 'You should definitely go to law school. You should absolutely — oh, you were born to be a lawyer. I see how you think and how you articulate, and you need to be a lawyer.' I would never have thought of it. And, remember, this is a kid that wasn't even supposed to go to college."

"Little did I know that three of the four law schools that I applied to, my chances of getting in were very, very slim, but I didn't know that, so I didn't know I should choose a safety school or any of that concept. I just threw my application stuff there. And I got a call from Yale, and it was from one of the recruiters at Yale, and they said, 'Where else did you apply?' and I said, 'Well, Harvard,' because I thought they were one and the same. And they said, 'Oh, you don't want to go to Harvard.' Now, I hadn't heard from Harvard yet. So they said, 'You don't want to go to Harvard; you want to come here.' I'm like, 'Well, why?' and they said, 'Well, first of all, we're much smaller. Harvard has an entering class of 500, we have an entering class of 150. And second, Harvard has this huge — the grades are hugely competitive. Everyone is trying to be number one in their class. At Yale your first year, it's pass/fail. We take all that competition out and get you to just concentrate on learning to be a lawyer, and we're just the best school; we're number one in the country, so that's why you need to come here.' So before I ever heard from any other school, I said yes. I just said yes."

I clear my throat. "And criminal defense? How did that start?" I ask Juanita.

"Well, I knew I wanted to — this is going to sound a bit cold and calculating — I knew that I wanted to do trial work, and the only way you're going to do that is either as a prosecutor or a defender. And there was no thought in my mind that I could ever be a prosecutor."

"Why not?" I ask.

"Because I would be prosecuting people for things that I myself might do on any given day or my friends might do. Like drug crimes, for example. It's insane that people were

7

going away for these really lengthy periods of time for these small drug offenses. So, it just — my heart was definitely on the defense side, and I didn't — to be honest with you, I really didn't know how much until I became a defender, and then I fell hard. The injustices that I saw were outrageous."

"You said you fell hard," I say. "It sort of sounds like you fell in love with it, Juanita."

"I not only fell in love with it, but I fell in love with the cause of it, which is what happened when I saw these 15 young men all handcuffed together, terrified when I joined the federal defender's office, and I realized that I was their only voice. Without me, there was no one to speak for them. And when I realized that, I realized that this was my calling, that this was what I really needed to do." She pauses "At least for a long time that is what I did." She sounds nostalgic. She nods at me and goes to sit down. There is applause.

I go back to the podium. "Our next speaker is an assistant federal defender in Chicago, Amanda Bashi." Amanda walks to the podium. She is willowy, red-headed, and looks like total class, like she came from serious money. The opposite is true I know, and I bet some of the audience will be surprised when they find out more about her.

"**Amanda Bashi** graduated law school in 2011," I continue. "At first, she went into private practice, doing criminal defense with her close friend from law school, Katie Kizer. Then, she was hired at the federal defender's office in Chicago. She is the winner of the Illinois Association of Criminal Defense

Lawyers young lawyer award in 2015. Please help me welcome Amanda Bashi!"

"Good morning, everyone," she begins. "I'm 29, and I grew up in Victorville, California, which is a small town about halfway between Los Angeles and Las Vegas, and I think growing up there is actually a big part of why I ended up where I am workwise. Actually, for a small semirural town, it was pretty diverse, and I didn't recognize how lucky we were to have that at that time because, to me, that was just how the world was. Only when I went to college did I realize how different other places were, and I remember vividly being in college at the University of California at San Diego. Within the first couple weeks of being there, I talked to numerous people who would say, 'Oh, how many people from your high school came here?' And I didn't really understand what they meant. They were asking how many people from my graduating class came to the same college I went to, and my answer was zero because so few people from my high school went to college. I didn't really realize that that wasn't the norm or that that wasn't the case at a lot of other places. So my first year of college was very eye opening about where I grew up compared to where other people grew up."

"Victorville, when you drive through it on the freeway, may take about 30 seconds, and you're going to look around and just see mostly desert and a lot of chain restaurants. It's actually grown a lot since I've moved from there. If you drive into the town, it's a mid-sized town. It was, at least when I was there, over 100,000 people, but not by much. It's kind of a weird place. A lot of people live there because they work in LA or San Bernardino where it's a little more expensive to try and live. They also built a pretty significant amount of public housing in Victorville, so I think that was a big incentive for people to move from these more expensive, more southern towns, to Victorville. There's also a federal prison there, so there's a significant population of people that work at the prison."

"Can you tell us about your family, Amanda?" I ask.

Amanda flips back her hair. "Well, my dad is an air traffic controller. He grew up in a lot of cities, but mostly in Arizona, in Phoenix. He joined the Air Force right out of high school and then went to work as an air traffic controller, which is, actually, I think one of the best jobs you can get without a college degree. He's been doing that ever since, so it's been almost 30 years. And my mom got a job right out of high school working in a public parks and rec office as a secretary and then worked her way up to grant writing, and she still does that, too, in a different city. But they have both had public jobs my whole life and pretty much their whole careers. Then I have one sister who is six years younger than me, and she went to school to do hair and makeup and stuff. So we took very different tracks, she is a hairdresser now."

"Can you tell us a little bit about being a first generation college student? Whose idea was it for you to go to college?" I ask Amanda.

"It was my dad's definitely. But I really — I think he was more doing it because he was afraid for me about opportunity and where I would end up if I stuck around Victorville. You know, if I didn't do college, what was I going to do? A lot of people who stick around, they end up working and being happy, some of them end up with addictions, some of them end up struggling with families that they weren't able to plan for, and I think he just really thought college was something that could keep me away from all of that. For me, I started thinking about it very early on because of him. And once I got it set in my head that that's what I was going to do, there really wasn't any other option. I was also really excited to leave. And college for me was a way out. It seemed so exciting. You see it on TV and it looks like so much fun. So I really — I wasn't not going to go to college."

"Did you have an idea that law was in your future, or is that something that came later?" I ask.

"No," she says ruefully shaking her head. "I actually applied as pre-med, and then I got there and saw the prerequisites and thought that I had better think twice about that after the first quarter or two. I didn't do very well my first year of college, not because I wasn't working hard, but because I wasn't prepared."

"In what way do you feel that you weren't prepared? You just hadn't had as hard classes, you didn't have as much independent work? Was it the quality of your high school?"

Amanda nods. "Yeah. I think, particularly with writing, I look back at what we were asked to do, assignments in high school, writing assignments, and then compare them to what people, what my college friends, were asked to do in high school. It sounds like a joke when I tell them what we were asked to do, because it would be even as a senior in high school, write a three-page paper, and every paragraph has to have five sentences, you know, that kind of assignment. And my colleagues were writing about these kind of more theoretical papers where they got to really think about things and be critical, and I didn't feel like our high school gave us an opportunity to think critically and then put that critical thought into writing. I think that was because the school was geared toward people that weren't going to go past high school, for the most part."

The Feminine Sixth: Women for the Defense

"When I got to college, I was shocked at how, well, ignorant people were about things. I remember taking a class called Hip-Hop in Modern America, and we talked a lot about race in that class. I didn't have any friends in that class. I remember a student, a white student, raising her hand and arguing with our professor, who was a black male, about how her roommate is black and she loves her, so are we really still talking about race and racism? And I got so upset that I just had to get up and leave. I found out from a classmate at the next class that the professor just ended the class because he couldn't bear to go on, I guess, that day. And I don't blame him. But that's where a lot of students were coming from, so it really upset me."

"I took a social movements class, and one of the speakers was a very famous lawyer from the Innocence Project in California. And my professor framed the conversation as an anti-death penalty movement, this is one piece of it. So it led me to look more into that, and I ended up applying and getting an internship at the Death Penalty Information Center in Washington, D.C., where I got to live for four or five months during undergrad. While I was there, we met with various allies and other organizations, anti-death penalty organizations, and it was when Troy Davis's case was getting a lot of attention. I got to meet his sister. Talking with her and hearing from her and just watching how that case played out, even into law school, when I was there in D.C. — that was when I decided I want to do criminal defense work."

Amanda pauses for a moment. "Somewhere in there I knew I was going to apply to law school, but I wasn't sure exactly where I would head. I had an inkling it would be criminal defense, but being in D.C. for externships and working with the organizations we worked with and meeting the people I met, I felt very comfortable after that saying that the reason

I'm going to law school is to be a criminal defense lawyer, and I specifically want to work on death penalty cases."

"Now, in fairness, I should disclose that you ended up going to law school where I happened to be a teacher." I grin in Amanda's direction. "Could you talk about how that happened?"

"Well, I decided that all the schools I got into I was going to go visit because I had never lived outside of California. It was going to be a big move no matter where I went, and I kind of had a singular desire with what I wanted to do with my law degree. So I decided to really be an advocate for myself and find a place that was going to give me the exposure and the kind of access to academics and legal professionals that were great thinkers in the area I wanted to be in, which was criminal defense. So at every school I visited, I told them to 'show me your social justice programs, show me your criminal defense clinics. Show me these opportunities when I come because this is why I'm coming.' So when I came to DePaul, I was shown around. And I saw the *Journal for Social Justice* executive editor, I saw a panel that was happening that day on immigration policy, and then she took me to meet you. And at the time, you were working on the Casey Anthony case."

That was a hell of a case, I remember. I can't say I ever want to go to Orlando, Florida again. "I was crazed," I comment.

"You *definitely* were crazed. And I just remember walking into an office full of students who looked busy but so excited to be doing the work they were doing. Everybody was working. Nobody looked up when we opened the door, nobody gave us the time of day. And I actually really liked that." We both laugh, so does the audience.

The Feminine Sixth: Women for the Defense

"You know, Shea, who was my guide that day, walked me over to you and said, 'Andrea, this is Amanda. She's an admittee; she's considering coming here.' And you said, 'Amanda, if you want to do death penalty work, I'd be very excited to have you. But, unfortunately, right now I'm swamped with working on this case, and I can't really sit down and talk to you more than that.' I really liked that because, to me, that said — and, first of all, I already knew who you were, so it wasn't like I needed to hear a whole lot from you — but to me it just said, 'I'm prioritizing my client. If you want to join this team, look around, you can. But I don't have much more time for you other than that.' Also, I liked that all the students were also as crazed as you were. You guys were all on the same team, and no other school showed me that, anything close to that. So leaving there, I was, like, 'Done.' My decision was made. DePaul and criminal defense."

The audience applauds, and Amanda goes to sit at the table. I nod at Crystal, who is next alphabetically. "Now it is my pleasure to introduce Crystal Marchigiani. Crystal is a career public defender, starting out in California, but then coming to Illinois for the most excellent of reasons — love! She joined

the Cook County Public Defender's office in Chicago when I was still there, and became a member of and ultimately chief of the Homicide Task Force. She retired from the public defender's office a little less than a year ago. Please help me welcome **Crystal Marchigiani!**"

"I was born in Sacramento, California, and I'm the eldest grandchild and the oldest of two daughters. My sister is five years younger than me. Growing up, my grandfather kind of lived all over the place because he was a preacher, but eventually my gram settled next door to us in a small apartment. My aunt lived down the street with my cousin, who was like my elder sister, and my mom and dad and sister and I lived in what everybody called the 'Big House' on the corner." Crystal laughs a bit ruefully. "It was only big because we were all really poor. It was just a small, bungalow-style house with two small bedrooms and my mom and dad's bedroom. We were all really poor."

"The man I call my dad is actually my stepfather, but he married my mom when I was two, so he's my dad. For all intents and purposes, he's my dad. He's the guy who raised me. My mom, when I was real young, my mom was a waitress, my dad was a bartender. My mom worked dinner shifts at kind of the steakhouses and restaurants in Sacramento, for what that's worth. At some point, my dad was the sergeant at arms for the state Senate, which he said was like being the opposite of a bouncer because he would go into the bars when the senate was ready for a vote and get everybody out so they could vote. They were definitely blue-collar people, they were definitely lower economic scale people, but somehow the people they knew were really interesting and were always around. So it was interesting growing up. My dad died when I was 15, and my mom died three years ago, three or four years ago."

"Your dad died when you were 15? That's very young to lose your father," I say.

Crystal swallows. I think to myself she looks so put together, so elegant, yet her roots are so *not* that.

"I think in the lore of the family, it was the worst thing that ever happened," she continues. "But personally — actually, my dad died in October, my grandfather died the following February, and my best friend's older sister, so you know how

15

that is when you're a kid, your best friend's older sister is like your older sister — committed suicide two months later. So it was shocking how much loss there was."

"My sister was ten, which, when my dad died, I sort of thought to myself, well, I'm 15, I can deal with it, whether I could or I couldn't. What I thought was really unfair is that she was ten and devastated. And in our family, the other dynamic is that she and my mom were very similar, so they did not get along at all. And inside my family it was a well-known fact she was my father's girl. And I don't mean that he didn't love us both. I mean that she tagged along, and he liked to have her tag along, and he always called her 'Little Lorraine;' my mom's name was Lorraine. We probably all were in complete denial, but when I look at it now, I think, oh, my God, my mother was 40 years old; that's so young. She lost her best friend, to say nothing of the man who she really expected to spend the rest of her life with. And they had a very affectionate, intellectual, romantic relationship. They had it all. And she lost him and she was 40 years old. She was bereft. I didn't see it at the time because we were all focused on ourselves. But now I realize I'm sure that she thought, 'How am I going to raise these two without him?'"

"Do you remember when it was you decided you wanted to be a lawyer, when did that happen, and why?" I ask, after a moment. There had been a palpable hush in the audience.

"I was nine," she responds.

"Good heavens," I say. I decided when I was 15, pretty much, but nine? "Tell us about that?"

Crystal grins. "Actually, the story is kind of a cool story, and I want to do my mentor justice. One of the people that was always around in my parents' lives, not just the parties, but in their lives, was one of the most prestigious African American lawyers, men, in north Sacramento, and he was a guy who worked on every kind of law there was, including opening up banks and opening up housing to African Americans, and he did it all really quietly. There was never any fanfare and never any fuss, and he never got told no. He just worked really hard. But his love was criminal defense. So here's what I remember about him before I knew all these other things."

"I was nine years old and he would come by my parents' house — his office was somewhere between my parents' house and downtown, so he kind of had to travel to get to our house, but he would always come by at 11 o'clock at night, basically a night owl, and he worked really late at his office. My parents would have a pot of coffee on, believe it or not, for him, and he had his own coffee cup at our house. His name was Douglas Greer, Douglas R. Greer. He made me want to be a lawyer, but it didn't seem possible."

"My family couldn't help. If my grandmother could send me $50 every once in a while, I was really grateful, and it really hurt her. She just didn't have the kind of money that people have now to spend on their kids or the kind of money that my friends spend on their kids now. I thought, I'm never going to get there anyway, I'm never going to be a lawyer because this is just too hard. I've got four more years. I thought, maybe I'll just put school on the back burner and I'll go back. I thought all of that stuff. And I was talking to my mom who was panicking, and she said, 'You wait there,' and in the next 15 minutes, Douglas called me. And he wasn't nice. He basically told me that the work that I wanted to do was really hard, and if I wasn't willing to put in the work it took to get there, then

The Feminine Sixth: Women for the Defense

I probably wouldn't be a very good lawyer anyway. I mean, it was really that kind of conversation."

"That sounds tough," I say.

"Well, he wasn't a guy who had kids or knew very much about what to do with them, and I was probably as close to a kid as he was ever going to have, and he wasn't very good at it. But it worked. I guess he made me mad maybe. I think I got pissed off, like, 'Fine, I'll show you.' I think I always expected to get out of law school and go to work with Douglas, and then I didn't because I interned with the public defender's office, and that's a calling. And when you are right for the public defender's office, that's all you want to do, and that's what I wanted to do. And that is what I have done (and loved) for my whole career."

Crystal returns to her seat.

Photo Credit: eedahahm

"Our next presenter is **Huma Rashid**. Huma is in private practice with Raymond Wigell and Associates, doing criminal defense work. She is near the beginning of her career; she has been practicing about five years. And just wait until we get into the nature of some her criminal defense work later in the discussion."

Huma walks to the podium and lowers the microphone. Then she lowers it a bit more. She is about five feet tall. Maybe. "I was born in Boston, in the suburbs of Boston, in Mattapan, so about 15, 20 minutes from downtown proper. I was born in 1986. Both of my parents are immigrants from Pakistan."

Huma's chin goes up as she says this. There is remembered pain there, and I can see her looking for that "uh-oh" reaction.

"They were born and raised in Karachi, and my dad had come over to Chicago in 1971. He went to school here, he worked here, and then he went back in the early '80s. He and my mom got married. They'd been friends since childhood, they'd lived on the same street. My dad was really good friends with my mom's older brother. Then they moved to America after they got married, to Boston, because my mother got a scholarship to complete her Ph.D. at Boston University while teaching some additional courses there. Then we moved to Chicago. My mother had always had a dream that her kids would be educated at an Islamic school. We were in Chicago for my dad's cousin's wedding, and she happened to meet a man who was the principal of a local Islamic school, and he found out that she studied economics and had a math background, so he offered her a job at the College Preparatory School of America in Lombard. It was still fairly relatively new at that point. I think it had only been started in 1992 officially."

"We learned all the normal subjects, so English, history, math all that stuff. But as a foreign language, we had Arabic instead of, like, Spanish or French. We had an extra period for Islamic studies. We had a Quran period I think, like, once a week where we memorized portions of the Quran in Arabic. Because we pray five times a day as Muslims, there was a set time for prayer, for the midday prayer, on pretty much all school days, so it was kind of like a recess, where instead of going to play at recess, everyone went down to the gym, there were prayer services, and we went right back to classes. I remember that the boys' uniform was always a white dress shirt and blue slacks, and the girls' uniform was in elementary a blue jumper, and a hijab, h-i-j-a-b, which is the veil worn over the hair, that was kind of optional. No one really cared

The Feminine Sixth: Women for the Defense

if you wore it or not, it was if you wanted to, if your family wanted you to. It was up to you. But when you hit 6th grade, that's when the — grades 6 through 12 were on the upper floor of the building, it was a two-story building, and that was when the girls' uniform became a full-length jilbab, j-i-l-b-a-b, which is a full-length robe, full sleeves, and a white hijab, and that covered the hair. A niqab, n-i-q-a-b, which is the veil that covers the entire face except for the eyes, was not required. In fact, I only knew one or two girls that ever wore it, so that was not part of the culture."

"Then in law school, I discovered another aspect of Islam that I hadn't known of before, it's Sufism. People might think of it as the Buddhism of Islam. It's very much steeped in ritual, but it also incorporates a lot of other spiritual aspects that people might not delve into as deeply otherwise. So that kind of developed through law school. I just read a lot more, I practiced a lot more, and it continued after I graduated law school when I started working."

"I ended up applying to law schools because my dad was probably right and that law was probably more secure than academia which had been my first thought, and that's kind of how — I hate using the phrase 'immigrant mind-set,' but that's basically what it is. My parents' definition of success and what they'd always pushed on me, or impressed upon me, since I was a kid was kind of two-fold: It was success in terms of financial stability, not so much wealth, but stability, and a respected position. And that was, for my dad, certainly a lawyer."

I interrupt here. "Huma, women haven't been around in law, particularly criminal defense, in any numbers for very long. So it's also interesting that you ended up doing this work, which I know we will hear more about because — and this, again, is probably just my prejudice, but the view from the

20

outside of a Muslim is that they're discriminating towards women, that women are not allowed to do very much. So it's interesting that your dad pushed you into the profession — albeit perhaps not with criminal defense in mind."

Huma is nodding, and her slightly impish smile is visible. "I give my dad a lot of credit for that because a lot of Muslim parents, when they push their daughters into careers like doctors or lawyers, they're looking at it from the perspective of this will make my child more marriageable. She'll be more attractive to a male suitor if he knows that she's a doctor or a lawyer, someone with earning potential. That's the reality of it. I've seen it play out in my social circles, women my age. It's unfortunate and I'm disgusted by it, but it's part of the reality in our social group. And because of that, criminal defense isn't the field of law that a lot of parents think of if they push their daughters into law."

"As to criminal defense, well I read a book my very first semester called *Defending the Damned: Inside Chicago's Cook County Public Defender's Office*, by Kevin Davis. It was a book that a friend of mine also in law school recommended to me. She read it, she loved it, and so I read it. I read it expecting to be totally grossed out, totally turned off, but, nevertheless, wanting to expose myself to a field of law that I didn't know much about. Obviously you were featured in that book, so were several other attorneys. I read the whole thing and I found it so compelling, and that's the only word I can use for it, because obviously the subject matter is deeply disturbing, a lot of the cases mentioned there would offend most people. They're horrible, because obviously those were cases where people were eligible for the death penalty because of the seriousness of the alleged crimes. When I finished the book, it was so compelling that I thought that if you're going to be an attorney, you should be an attorney that makes a huge

The Feminine Sixth: Women for the Defense

difference, and I couldn't think of any kind of attorney that made more of a difference than a defense attorney."

"Tell me about how you ended up with Wigell and Associates," I ask.

"Well finding a job was very hard, any job. Perhaps my name had something to do with it? Finally, in October, about six months after graduation, I saw a listing for a criminal defense attorney in Olympia Fields who wanted an associate with zero to three years' experience. And I thought, perfect, that's me, zero years." There is laughter in the audience. "I had no idea where Olympia Fields was, and I was feeling a little dejected and I was, like, well, why should I even apply, he'll just reject me like everyone else. So I didn't apply. A week later, the listing was still on my law school's e-mail blast. I thought, 'Well, he hasn't found anyone in a week, so why not? I might as well.' It was with Raymond Wigell. And he gave me a call back and he said, 'Why don't you come in for an interview?' I came in, and you came up in the first interview because he mentioned you somehow in one of his cases that he was working on." Huma nods in my direction.

"We were working on a death penalty case together," I reply.

"So he mentioned that, and my face just lit up," she continues. "He asked me if I knew you, and I said, 'No, but I want to.'" There is more laughter. "So he brought me in for a second interview and then he unofficially hired me. But for my third interview, he had me shadow a two-day felony trial in Markham, and I was responsible for taking notes during the trial for the motion for a new trial after one we lost. I just spent that whole trial with him and he hired me right after that. I started a couple days later, and I've been with him since. So I had a year and a half of absolutely nothing, nothing. No callbacks, no interviews, nothing. And the first one was the right one. It is still the right one, and I am committed to criminal defense." Huma kind of waves at the audience and takes her seat.

"It is my pleasure to introduce the next panelist, Cynthia Roseberry," I say.

Photo Credit: Rebecca Haehnle, Parlour Salon

"**Cynthia W. Roseberry** just finished serving as Project Manager for Clemency Project 2014 since its inception. Clemency Project 2014 was a partnership among the National Association of Criminal Defense Lawyers, American Civil Liberties Union, the American Bar Association, Families Against Mandatory Minimums, and the Federal Community and Public Defenders created in response to Deputy Attorney General James Cole's request to the legal profession to provide pro bono assistance for clemency to federal prisoners who would likely receive a shorter sentence if they were sentenced today, among other criteria. She is now the Executive Director of the Council for Court Excellence in Washington, D.C."

"Before joining the Project, Cynthia served as Executive Director of the Federal Defenders of the Middle District of Georgia, Inc. For more than ten years she practiced federal and state criminal defense in Georgia, then Cynthia founded the Misdemeanor Clinic, and taught Advanced Criminal Procedure and co-taught in the Death Penalty Clinic at DePaul University College of Law in Illinois. Cynthia earned her B.S. from Wilberforce University in Wilberforce, Ohio, and her J.D. from Georgia State University College of Law in Atlanta, Georgia. Cynthia is a founding board member of the Georgia Innocence Project and a past president of the

The Feminine Sixth: Women for the Defense

Georgia Association of Criminal Defense Lawyers. Please help me welcome Cynthia Roseberry!"

Cynthia walks to the podium. She is dressed beautifully, if non-traditionally, in a short cap-sleeved blue dress with leather trim, is wearing very high heels which I admire, but couldn't wear. She gets to the podium and squares her shoulders.

"I was born and reared in Atlanta, and I'm the youngest of five children. My parents, there was an eight-year difference between them in age. My father was actually born in 1913, which I think is interesting. I was a late-in-life child, of course, for my parents. I think I saw in the neighborhood in which I was reared, which was a predominantly African American neighborhood on the west side of Atlanta, just a lot of sadness in that neighborhood. My father went to Morehouse, he was college-educated. My mother was not, and many of the folks in our neighborhood were not. So I saw a lot of sadness in them and I saw a lot of folks who just didn't have a voice. Even my father, if you think about it, in 1933 he would have been a 20-year-old college-educated black man in the south, and so even he didn't have a voice. I think he studied biology, I am not sure if he ever worked in the field he was educated in."

"I'm told he was a professor. I don't know a lot about him; he died when I was 17, turning 18, and my parents had divorced when I was about 12. So we didn't spend a lot of time together after they divorced, and he was sick. He was an alcoholic. So I didn't get to learn a lot about him, but I think he studied biology. But I know he spoke German and sang opera and all these kinds of things. My mother was not college-educated, but she had a license to be a cosmetologist, she had a real estate license, she was an entrepreneur at one time, had a soul food restaurant, and she says when I was eight years old, I told her that I was going to be her lawyer, her corporate lawyer."

"Seriously? When you were eight?" I ask. "That's awfully young."

Cynthia nods vigorously. "When I was eight. I have no idea where that came from. I guess just being around her and her company and watching that grow, somehow I must have decided, 'I'm going to be your corporate lawyer.' So ultimately when I went to law school, it was after she passed away, because I wanted to honor that promise that I made to her to become a lawyer, although not a corporate lawyer. I was kind of nerdy, and I remember in my neighborhood if you used proper English, you stood out, so they nicknamed me 'Ms. Proper.' Well, it's funny because my father addressed us all that way. I was Ms. Cindy; that was my nickname. Everybody else was Ms. Mila, Ms. Derica, Ms. Dethonia, Mr. Vernon. And I think about that now, and I think he probably did that because as a child he probably couldn't be referred to as 'Mr.' My sisters taught me to read, and I loved to read. So when I went to school, English wasn't a second language that I was learning. In my neighborhood, most people spoke standard English as a second language, the first being some form of Ebonics. So I got picked on a little bit. And then I remember another story where the bullies were going to beat me up and I negotiated with them, and said, 'Listen, don't beat me up, but sit next to me when we have a test and I'll help you with the test.' And that's how I maneuvered. One of my teachers found out and she would sit me off to the side so that nobody could get help from me." The audience laughs.

"My desire and intention to go to college was very unusual in my neighborhood. Very few people had college-educated parents, very few people even aspired to go to college. College was a wonderful experience because our professors expected a lot of us and were accessible to us. You know, Wilberforce is a typical HBCU, (Historically Black College or

The Feminine Sixth: Women for the Defense

University) in that it admitted people who would likely not have been admitted into a number of other schools. A lot of the folks have gone on to lead very different lives because of that. So it saved a lot of lives. It's small, underfunded, it's controlled by the A.M.E. church. And if you know the history of those church-run schools like Fisk and Morris Brown, they have considerable financial difficulties. We had parties in the student union like everybody else, and just about everybody else was just as poor as I was. I remember every blue moon my mother might have five dollars that she would put in an envelope and send to me. I had work study and student aid, you know, everybody had student aid, and we were getting all these loans that we had no idea we were going to have a hard time paying back, but need them to get through school."

"I remember moving off campus because I recognized that if I lived in the city, I was a resident, which meant that I could get some help. So I got food stamps when I moved out, and I had enough to eat that way. I would buy fish and make fish sandwiches and sell the sandwiches and have money to wash my clothes and to get deodorant and soap and things like that. That's how I made it. So it taught me how to survive on my own and taught me to believe in myself a lot. It was a good school. And even now when I go back for high school reunions, out of the 300 or so folks who graduated, you can count the number people who went on to get an undergraduate degree on one hand, and I'm one of them. And I am the only lawyer in our class. After college I got married and moved to Germany with my former husband. I had been there about three years when I got the feeling that I needed to come home. I came home, and my mother was sick and in the hospital, and she died shortly after I came home." Cynthia stops, and swallows hard.

"I'm so sorry," I say. I knew her mother was gone, but, well it comes back hard sometimes. It certainly does for me, even though it has been almost seven years since I lost my mom.

"Thank you," Cynthia says quietly. "That's when I decided I was going to go to law school to make that promise to her. She died in 1990. But it was those without a voice that I was most interested in representing. I tried doing entertainment law, but I just was drawn to, and remain drawn to, criminal defense. I like the work, for its spirit, and frankly," she grins. "I like the fight too!"

Cynthia takes her seat and Cyndy Short gets up. "It's my pleasure to next introduce you to Cyndy Short," I begin.

"**Cyndy Short** graduated from law school in 1987 in St. Louis, Missouri. Working her first position as a lawyer in a small labor law firm, she was appointed to represent a young poor woman the federal government accused of attempting to assassinate Jesse Jackson during his 1988 presidential campaign. This experience changed the course of her practice and she dedicated most of the next 15 years of her career to the representation of poor people as a public defender in Kansas City. She served in the Kansas City office of the Missouri Public Defender first in the trial division, then in the capital litigation division, where she served as head of that office for nearly a decade. The capital division worked exclusively for those indigent defendants facing the death penalty at trial. Her job: On many occasions, to prove their innocence. And in all cases, to save their lives. Cyndy's achievements for her clients are too numerous to mention, having tried well in

The Feminine Sixth: Women for the Defense

excess of 100 jury trials. But I have a favorite: very early in her career, when a jury — angered by the treatment of her client — acquitted that client and demanded an apology from the police and prosecutors for their wrongdoing!" I shake my head in wonder. "Please help me welcome Cyndy Short!"

Cyndy walks to the podium. She has a style I would call Bohemian professional. She is wearing an interesting print jacket-like cape over black slacks and a shirt.

"I am the oldest of five children. My father is Tom Short, my mother is Carol Short. My mother and dad met in New York City. And my dad was actually from Moberly, Missouri, which is a rural area. He was an only child, and his mother really wanted him to have a big society life. So when he wanted to go to the University of Missouri to play football, she wanted him to go to Notre Dame, and she won. He left Notre Dame and went into the Air Force, and the Air Force took him to New York City where my mother was working for CBS, and on a blind date they met and very quickly fell in love and decided to get married. But that changed the course of my father's career because he had seen himself as a prosecutor in his small town, and then a judge in his small town, and then the governor of the state, and she saw the small town and said, 'Uh, no.' So instead, he went into aerospace with his law degree but never practiced law, and they were part of the Apollo program, so we lived in Texas during the Apollo program."

"So I was the first of their five children, and I was born in New Jersey in 1961. During my childhood, my parents, we moved as if we were in the military. So through my childhood, I was in nine different schools before high school, mostly Texas and California and then Canada. As I grew up, I really was always pointed in the direction of the law by my dad almost as if it was, 'I didn't do it, and so this seems like something you should do.' But more than dad, it was my grandmother. She and her mother owned a very large dress store in Moberly, Missouri, and she talked to me a lot about going to an all-women's college in Columbia and then being an attorney, something that she didn't get to do. She didn't get to college and she didn't get to go to law school, obviously. But she saw a much different kind of lawyer than what I turned out to be I promise you."

"I really was not an extrovert at all. I would have died to get up in front of anybody, you know, in high school or middle school. I was self-conscious, you know, like all girls are. I didn't find myself particularly attractive. I was at times overweight, so I had a lot of those struggles that you know, girls have. I was the favored child inside my house, you know, because I was the good girl. I did everything right. I had the good grades, I was never a problem, I didn't lead, in terms of being the leader of the five kids, I did not go astray as others would, as they would move down the line. So I was the good girl."

The audience laughs appreciatively. I find myself wondering how many of them were the "good" child too. I certainly was, ironically.

"You talked a little bit about not feeling confident about how you look, and I have to say I'm sort of surprised because you're gorgeous and you come across as very confident in your looks. So did that change as you got older? Did it just stop worrying you?" I ask. Looks are an issue for everyone, but for women particularly.

Cyndy cocks her head to the right for a moment. "I think it definitely changed as I got older. I think sports for me, and, also, I went to an all-girls school in college. There was a confidence

The Feminine Sixth: Women for the Defense

that gave me in terms of, I think, other competencies that I had, and I was very well integrated into that environment."

"You said earlier that you weren't 'supposed' to do criminal defense. How did that happen?" I ask.

"Well I was at a small firm, and I was on the appointment list, and on a Friday afternoon that call came for me, the magistrate's clerk said they had a case, and it was a prisoners' rights case and I was disappointed; I wanted a criminal case. Kind of naive, but that's what I wanted. And about 30 minutes later she called me back and they were kind of in a panic, and she said, 'It's Friday afternoon,' so I guess that's why they called me back as opposed to finding a competent attorney, and said, you know, 'We have an emergency. Would you take a different appointment? Are you okay with a criminal case instead of a prisoners' rights case?' And I said, 'Yes, I am.' And she said, 'Well, we have got this couple from southern Missouri and they are white supremacists.' And then she said that they possessed an automatic weapon."

"So here's a girl from the city, never have I touched a gun. I don't know anything about white supremacists. Things were going through my head, like, 'is that itself a crime?'" The audience laughs appreciatively. "And then she says that they were being charged with attempting to assassinate Jesse Jackson, who, at the time, was running for president. It's kind of a big first case. But somehow I still said yes, then I hang up and I'm literally shaking like a leaf. Then I think, well, there's a husband, so somebody else is going to be appointed, and that person will actually be competent, and I'll go to that person and figure out what I'm supposed to do. The person that they appointed was another guy from my law school class, and he and I had done the seminar class together. We had been partners in the course, and guess who did all the work in that class? So I had recently been to a seminar, a federal seminar, where a guy named Art Margulis says to the group of young lawyers, 'If you ever find yourself appointed in a federal case and you really feel like you don't know which way is up, call me. I would be happy to help you.' So I called Art."

Cyndy looks over at me. "That's one of the things about us." She means criminal defense lawyers.

"Yes," I agree. "We all help each other."

Cyndy continues, "And so when we finished that case, she ended up taking a plea to the possession of the weapon, but not to the attempt to assassinate. And very shortly after that, we had delivered to him her petition for divorce. And here's the other weird thing about that case, Andrea: It was right when the guidelines that we are finally getting rid of slowly thank goodness — came in. I actually argued my only case in front of the Eighth Circuit, in that case arguing for a departure. It was one of the first cases ever argued under the guidelines in 1989."

"Cyndy, for those of the audience who don't know, we had mandatory sentencing guidelines in federal court that basically were a mathematical formula. If a judge didn't give that sentence, the judge had to explain why. So that is what you are talking about here?"

Cyndy nods. "That's right."

"So I quit the labor law job cold when this case was over. I went down to the mall and got a job at a dress store — and started interviewing with the public defenders and the prosecutors both, and knew, again, that, my heart would be with the PDs, but I also felt like we got taught in law school,

The Feminine Sixth: Women for the Defense

well, you can do either side. And, fortunately for me, the PDs chose me before the prosecutors did, because that was the right place. I was meant to defend."

Cyndy returns to her seat as she is applauded. "We have three more fabulous women to meet," I tell the audience. "Next up is Christine Start."

"**Christine Mari Palma Start** is honored to be President of the Filipino Bar Association of Northern California. She is a Deputy Public Defender with Solano County Alternate Public Defender where she proudly represents indigent individuals charged with crimes from arraignment through jury trial and appeal. Christine's passion for public defense work sparked over ten years ago while working as a criminal defense investigator in Washington, D.C. Christine has been featured as a speaker and panelist at several 'Know Your Rights' community forums and educational events, and also sits on the Racial Justice Committee where she works. Christine serves as Co-Chair of the Minority Bar Coalition of the Bay Area and Advisory Board Member of the University Of San Francisco School Of Law Public Interest Foundation. Christine has what she describes as a 'side hustle' as a Certified Life Professional Coach and Energy Leadership Index — Master Practitioner called FireStarter Coaching. Christine practices yoga philosophy and meditation; she is on a mission to harmoniously integrate all of her life passions and to empower others to do the same. Christine you *know* you will have to tell us more about that! Please help me welcome Christine Start!"

"Well, as you probably can tell from that introduction, I'm Filipino. I grew up in a town called Union City, it's in California, and it's in the Bay Area. I pretty much grew up there my entire life. I stayed in the Bay Area for college. I went to UC Berkeley, I took a year off, and then I went to USF, University of San Francisco, for law school. I haven't really left the Bay Area other than my first real public defender gig. I was in Fresno for that part of time. But I returned back to the Bay Area. I've just been a home-grown Bay Area girl. I don't want to leave. My family, my family is very traditional. I'd say we're a very large family. Filipinos tend to roll pretty deep in terms of the number of people."

"When you say, 'traditional,' could you explain to us what you mean by that?" I ask.

"I think traditional in the sense that I grew up very — what's the — like, go to school, get an education, and don't be a bad person, be a good person. Actually, I didn't grow up very religious. I did go to catechism school, which is church school, on the weekends, but my parents didn't go to church. I don't know how that happened other than one of my really good friends, we had close family friends that were very religious. So maybe we're not a traditional Filipino family in the sense that we're not super Catholic. My mom, she's much more of a churchgoer now than she was when I was growing up. Also when I say, 'traditional,' I mean Filipino families are very big, so everybody's business is your business. Everybody's there at graduation, everybody's there at your birthday. You don't grow up in just this small, like, Mom, Dad, siblings. You grow up with everybody, kind of."

"Union City is close to 40 percent Filipino, so a lot of my friends were Filipino growing up, and they also had very large families as well. I think why it's such a big part of who

The Feminine Sixth: Women for the Defense

I am as a lawyer is because that was who supported me on this path because nobody in my family was a lawyer. I'm the first person in my family to even express interest in being a lawyer. So I didn't really have any role models. So I think what happened is when I decided I wanted to be a lawyer, which was at the end of my years at Cal in college, I was associated with a pre-law/pre-business group that was Filipino because the Filipino community at Cal was fairly large."

"What sparked my interest in law was I ended up doing this program called 'Cal in the Capital,' where you find an internship in Sacramento, and it's part of this whole program. One of the state assembly members taught it, and it was a really cool thing that they offered every summer for students. So I ended up getting a really cool job with Senator John Vasconcellos. This was the summer after my sophomore year at Cal. He was super liberal. He was the senator behind legalizing medical marijuana. He actually did a lot of prisoner rehabilitation work. So what sparked my interest? A couple things. But that was the beginning of my path, even though I don't think he ever was an attorney himself. I know he went to Santa Clara University, and he was very senior. He had been in the legislature before they did those term limits, so he had been a senator for eight to ten years, something like that. He was very known and just one of those, like, 'I'm going to do whatever the fuck I want to do,' you know, and, 'We need to lower the voting age to 14.' Really, the goal was similar to 16 so he pushed for 14 to get them talking. He was really into self-esteem and education on self-esteem, and I just thought he was really cool, a really cool dude."

"So what happened was I got assigned to work on a bill that — and I was in charge of calling all these different prison systems and looking at the different educational, psychosocial, and vocational programming that they offered in the prisons, because what he wanted to do, and what he was trying to do, was require that in all of the prisons that they offer this programming because he was a big believer in rehabilitation, and he wanted to give people something to do when they got out so that they didn't reoffend and recidivate. This was all brand-new stuff to me. But by working on that and contacting different prisons and talking to different programming representatives and just gathering all this data, it made me realize that, wow, there's this whole community of people that deserve these services, deserve therapy, you know, need the therapy and things like that, and we're not giving it to them while they're in prison, and they're just sitting in there. Then we're just going to let them back out in the community with nothing to do. So, of course, they're going to reoffend. That was the lesson that I got out of this job."

"So I was, like, I like this criminal aspect. What is it, you know? From that point on, I realized I had an interest in law, law and policy. So that was the start of me just kind of following this path to becoming a public defender. Then I applied to work for the Public Defender Service in Washington, D.C., as an investigator. I was, like, I'm just going to apply, let's see if I get it. It will be cool because I'll really explore D.C. I'm not going to be in the northwest quadrant, stuck there every day, like, 9:00 to 5:00. This is going to be some real — I'm going to see stuff, you know? So I said, 'Okay. Let me apply to this.' I actually got in, which was really cool, and I think I was one of eight criminal investigators who were all in college. And I worked — the case that I realized — I just thought it was cool, first of all. My partner that I was assigned, he was super Republican, but that didn't stop me. And if there had been any doubt that criminal defense was for me, it was gone after working with public defenders."

The Feminine Sixth: Women for the Defense

Christine turns to take her seat and I nod at Cynthia Stewart that it is her turn. How come there are so many Cynthias in this crowd, I wonder. Not to mention people whose names start with "C."

"**Cynthia A. Stewart** has her own law firm dedicated to obtaining the best possible outcome for people facing criminal charges in Mississippi. She has practiced in the area of criminal defense for more than 20 years. As a sole practitioner with a team of professionals supporting her, Cynthia enjoys a strong track record of success in both state and federal courts across the state. She has successfully tried a wide variety of criminal cases, including those involving the death penalty, capital murder, civil rights, aggravated assault, and fraud. She is particularly known for her solid history of achieving positive outcomes for people charged with a wide variety of crimes. Please help me welcome Cynthia Stewart!"

Cynthia walks to the podium, nodding and smiling at everyone as she does so. "I was born in Anniston, Alabama, to Mississippi parents. I came a little early, and my father worked for Alcohol, Tobacco, and Firearms as an undercover agent, so I was born under a false name. They had to stay down there until they could bring me home. On my wall at the office, I have my false birth certificate. My father died three years ago and I have the flag that came to me. It's kind of odd because while he was on the other side, so to speak, he had a remarkable ability to understand what I was doing and appreciate it and predict the outcome of controversial cases. He was my best public read."

"That's interesting Cynthia — he was law enforcement and you were defense, but he understood you well?" I observe.

"Yes. I know it seems odd." Cynthia definitely has the southern drawl. "We grew up in Jackson. My family is from the county where I now have my office. I live in Jackson. The county where I now have my office, when my father was growing up, they had a turkey farm out there. The Oklahoma Dust Bowl got them, and instead of going west, they came east and farmed the land. But by the time we came along — my father married relatively late and his parents had him relatively late — my grandparents were very elderly, and a lot of that land had been sold off, but it was still mostly rural. I remember there was always a lot of tension in the household, and looking back, I think a lot of it was because my father had an extremely sensitive job, probably not the greatest marriage in the world, and it kind of fell mostly to him to take care of his elderly parents. He was the breadwinner; my mother didn't work. So I can look back and see all the factors that caused it. My father had a very precarious, unpredictable temper. You could do something really simple and it would set him off. He didn't beat us; I don't mean that. He would get angry and it was a seething sort of anger that is intimidating, the slightest thing; or you could wreck the car and it was no big deal. You just never knew which way it was going to go. My mother was high-strung, and I'm not sure they were particularly well suited to one another."

"But looking back on it, I found it interesting that my father had a lot more influence on me, my sense of right and wrong, the sense to stand up and do what's right, than my mother did. My father always was an alcoholic, and it's how he dealt with his stress, and it's also very common, very common, among men in Mississippi, if not the South. Even now, I could reel off the names of several lawyers that have that bottle stuck up under," as she motions her arm under the table.

The Feminine Sixth: Women for the Defense

"I went to Millsaps for undergraduate and Washington University for law school. My then-husband was restless about what he wanted to do, and he decided he was going to go for his Ph.D., so I finished my last year at University of Michigan. At that time, I still planned to be an environmental lawyer. But because you had the guy that wrote the book there, Yale Kamisar — so I took that class. The passion he had for the rights of others just made me see law in a different way, and I think that more than anything sent me in that direction, to criminal defense."

I smile, I had the privilege of teaching on the same faculty with the redoubtable Professor Kamisar, and we became friends. I am going to have to be sure to tell him how he influenced this nearly accidental student.

"The other part of how I got into defense work came from the fact that before I got my law degree and for some months after, I worked for a civil rights organization in the Mississippi Delta, and I had to quit when I was pregnant with my first child. I didn't do pregnancies very well. But I liked representing the person who needed help, and so that's the work I chose." Cynthia goes to take her seat and the last of our panelists comes up, Lisa Wayne.

"**Lisa Monet Wayne** is an attorney in private practice in both state and federal courts around the country. She represents individuals and corporations in both the investigation phase and criminally accused capacity. Lisa was a Colorado State Public Defender for 13 years where she served as office head, training director, and senior trial attorney. She lectures nationally with the National Association of Criminal Defense Lawyers (NACDL), National Criminal Defense College (NCDC), National Institute of Trial Advocates (NITA), American Bar Association (ABA), and other legal organizations. Lisa is frequently quoted in print media such as the *Wall Street Journal*, *New York Times*, *Washington Post*, *Detroit Free Press*, and the *Associated Press* wire, and is often commenting on television. In 2005, Lisa was honored with the Robert C. Heeney Award, NACDL's most prestigious recognition, she is the Past President of NACDL, a trustee of the Foundation of Criminal Justice, and serves on numerous committees around criminal justice issues. Please help me welcome the amazing Lisa Wayne!"

"I was born in a very small village of maybe 110 people. My father was in Vietnam. They had never even seen black people in this village, and my mother didn't speak French. I had to learn right away how to make this constant adaptation to your environment, and my mother was that kind of woman. My mother had grown up in the Ida B. Wells housing projects in Chicago. My grandmother, Grand Coco, was Catholic, so my mother got educated because she went to Catholic schools in Chicago and lived with my grandmother, who lived in this small apartment. That's where my mom got raised. So, my Grand Coco was an extraordinary woman. She was married three times, she was incredibly beautiful, she was educated, and she worked within the civil service/government thing, so she made a decent living. She was quite the woman. She had married three times because she was way ahead of her time. I know that my mother's upbringing, and her feeling for those who were poor, influenced me too."

"Anyway, getting interested in law happened when I was about eight. So I remember being in the fourth grade and we lived on a military base. Everybody would know when

The Feminine Sixth: Women for the Defense

somebody's father had been killed because the protocol in the military is that these officers get out of a car and come to your door, and that's how you knew someone had died. We saw it a lot. It began to affect me because I remember thinking, 'When are they coming to our door? When are they going to say that my dad is dead?' I hadn't really thought at all about what I would be when I grew up or anything at that point. But then things changed."

"How?" I ask.

"Well, I was in fourth grade and I was acting out, which is totally opposite of the kind of student I was. I was a very good student, kind of a teacher's pet kid, I'm embarrassed to say, but I had begun to act out because of missing my father. So that was a crisis mode for me. And I remember my teacher, Ms. Gannon, one of the few teachers I remember, taking me out of class. She was young, and she had just bought a Cougar, a white Cougar, convertible, which was a big deal, and she put me in the car, which you would not be able to do, by the way, today without a parent permission slip, and took me on this drive and talked to me about what she thought I would be one day."

"Wow." I say. "She was the first to speak to you about a future?"

Lisa nods. "That just tells you how important teachers are. It had a huge impact on my life. And I totally changed the course of what was going on and we got through it and my dad came home. But, yeah, I remember that. And I've always wished that I could find her and tell her, and I've looked for her, but I've never been able to find her."

"What did she tell you about what she thought you would be one day?"

"You know, it's interesting, too, because Ms. Gannon was this youngish — in my mind, youngish — I don't really know how old she was, but when I look back, maybe in her 30s, kind of a hipster kind of teacher, white, and she said she thought I had the ability to be a leader, and she saw great things for me." Lisa continues, "She talked about politics, she talked about being a lawyer, she talked about things to her that seemed to be positions of influence that she thought I could be. And the fact that she told me that, made me start to think of myself that way."

"When I got out of law school, I went to the Colorado State Public Defender's office, which I just loved. But at a certain point, it became politically untenable to stay there. So I left, and I was fortunate because Jeralyn Merritt, who was a longtime federal lawyer, one of the first women, really, doing a lot of high-profile federal work, said to me, 'Come work over with me. I think you're great, you're the trial lawyer,' that she recognized she really wasn't; she was a motions lawyer, and she was of counsel to a larger firm, and it was a great setup. So I went with Jeralyn Merritt in Denver, and I learned so much with her. It was great. She took me on. She was not the true believer defender, she had never been a defender, so we had a very different mindset about many things. But she taught me the business and she taught me federal practice. There were no women in federal court when I started, and there still aren't very many and almost no women of color. She believed in me. She was great. She was one of the few women that were ahead of me that were good at mentoring younger women, because we're not good at that. We are not good at it. She never felt like I was invading her territory or was threatened by me or any of those things." Lisa shakes her head.

"That wasn't — my experience was women always helped me out," I reply. "But, of course, I was really at the very front of it and there were only a few women ahead of me. So that's part of it."

"If you talk to young women lawyers, they'll say women ahead of them are their worst detractors, women judges are the worst on the bench to us," Lisa says. "So it's just amazing to me to see the sisterhood in this room."

"Well, on that provocative note, we are done with our introductions. Let me suggest that everyone just stretch for a minute and we will go on to our next topic: emotions in our work."

CHAPTER TWO:
EMPATHY AND EMOTION IN OUR WORK

I call everyone to order, and they take their seats. We have put some microphones in the aisles so that when it's time, members of the audience can ask questions. "Welcome back," I begin. "We are now going to tackle one of the issues in our work, as criminal defense lawyers, and in particular as women." I look out and notice that I haven't quite gotten the audience interested.

"One of the experiences I have had, and I think a lot of us have had is that as women we are considered 'too emotional' to do this work, or we get told we are 'too involved.' If we fight hard for our clients on any particular issue, we get told we aren't 'ladylike,' or that we are that word that rhymes with 'witch.'" Now I see some smiling and nodding. "All of us have run into this in one form or another — in fact I have learned to anticipate that there will be jurors or judges who won't like me fighting, and who will hold it against me, and by extension, against my client." I pause for a moment.

"When I know there is going to be some fighting I will voir dire — ask jurors during the selection phase — about it. My default is to make folks laugh, so I will tell them that my grandmother used to tell me that I would 'never be a lady' because I was too opinionated and pushy (among other things). And then I will tell them that this has worried me less probably than

The Feminine Sixth: Women for the Defense

it might otherwise have because my grandmother used to eat corn on the cob, kernel by kernel with a fork and knife." There is laughter. "What many of us find is that we have to essentially get permission to do what men, particularly white men, already have permission for. So I would like to open up the floor for comments from the panel, and then we will take some questions from the audience." I turn to them. "Who would like to start?" I ask.

"I will," says Cyndy Short. "It wasn't until I attended the National Trial College that I was able to understand clearly that the ways in which we're asked to be attorneys in trials, there was a disconnection that was assumed, you know, that you don't get emotionally involved with the client and all that business. And instinctively that's what I was doing, but this gave me permission to do what I felt I should. This said, you know what? You're on the right track and you can even go further than where you were before."

"Do you feel that this is one of the places where men and women differ, or at least somewhat that women are more likely to be willing to be emotionally involved in their cases?"

"Yes," she replies.

"What about the stereotype of women lawyers falling in love with their clients and that type of thing? Did you feel that acknowledging some emotional connection to your client was a little bit easier for you to get to because you are a female, or not so much?" I ask.

Cyndy grins. "Oh. I think probably because I had been looking at the men as a way to figure out how to be, and now I knew that that was not the way to be, that they were disconnected from the clients, and this was, I think, distinctly female, and

I think that that would — which is why you see mitigation specialists, you know, dominate this idea of how we learn about who our clients are. But I was okay with that because I already was building connections with the clients in spite of the push to be 'objective.'"

"I already knew instinctively that the law really screwed our clients, that that was not the place for learning how to be the best lawyer, that you could call out the right numbers and say the right case name, but that, by itself was not going to win the day for the clients. What was going to win the day was the story. What was going to win the day was to walk in their shoes. So my energy changed in terms of, 'you only have so many hours in a day.' And it wasn't that I wasn't going to have people on my team that could fill that other lane, but in order for me to do what I wanted to do and for me to be successful at it, I was going to fill the lane that had to do with immersion in that person's life and in their story. I wanted to be places. I wanted to see an autopsy, I wanted to shoot a gun, I wanted to be in that person's house, and I wanted to go to the churches where my clients had gone to church. I wanted to see their grandfather preach a sermon and not just hear about it. You know what I mean? All of that changed, all of that energy changed. If I had a homeless client, I got out on the road and I started feeding the homeless and seeing where they lived. It took a while to feel that this was okay, and still a professional way to be."

"I am not sure I agree that it wasn't okay to connect," counters Cynthia Roseberry. "I always assumed you had to 'sit and rock' with your client."

"Can you explain that?" I ask her.

The Feminine Sixth: Women for the Defense

"What I mean is that taking care of the client is a part of the job. I can remember being in a sentencing in federal court, sitting with another woman, and there were a number of men, male lawyers, who went up with their clients. Of course their clients were getting these draconian sentences, and the lawyers seemed to be unaffected by it, and then I noticed that the other woman lawyer in the room, I mean, she clearly was affected by what her client got, and I think we women are fearless enough to risk caring. I think that men have to keep just that little bit of distance between them and the client to keep the client in a file instead of allowing them to come to life. And for us, our clients can come to life."

"What those who don't agree with you — men and women say — is that we burn out, and if we care too much, we can't see clearly and you need to have some distance. I'm sure you've heard this from male colleagues and probably some women colleagues, too," I respond.

"Sure," Cynthia replies. "But you know what? If I'm that defendant, I sure do want my lawyer caring for me. And if I would want that, that's what I should give. I don't want somebody speaking for me who doesn't care about the beat of my heart. I mean, how can they speak for you? I don't know. It just doesn't seem right to me. It doesn't seem right not to care. And the people who don't care burn out, too. You know, I've always taught my students, be the kind of lawyer you want your loved ones to have, that's important. And that's how — that's where you get the fire to look under that additional rock or to talk to that other witness, or one more time with your client. That's where that comes from, that caring."

Christine Start raises her hand, just a little tentatively. That makes me chuckle. "Christine?"

"I think part of the reason that I love being an advocate for people that can't voice things for themselves, either because they just don't have the knowledge or they don't have the power to or the resources to, I feel like I'm giving voice to the voice that I didn't have either. I'm only realizing that now because maybe that's why I'm such a rebel now, or whatever. I don't want to do what everybody else is doing, not because I really don't want to do what everybody else is doing, but it's just because I want to do what I want to do, and I'm tired of living up to everybody's expectations; especially those that come from my culture. I just want to live up to my own expectations and what my clients deserve. Yeah. So I don't know if that's what it is exactly. What I glean from just working with other people — other public defenders — is that we get involved, really involved with our cases. I don't see it as much with the male public defenders. You know, I talk to my boss and he'll tell me about things that bug him at night. I've been learning how to be emotionally detached but still very compassionate. Yeah, I think it's hard. There's a lot of emotion. You feel. You feel for your clients. How can you not?" She asks.

"Let me add something else into the mix here," I say. "I've heard from other women, if you express feelings or let your feelings show, then you're going too feminine or too weak or something. Is that something that you've felt at all, or not so much?"

Amanda Bashi speaks up. "I think women do feel that way. I don't particularly identify with that but I've heard from coworkers that they do feel that. I always try to affirm them because I think that showing emotion publicly is very courageous, just in a vacuum as a human act, I think showing emotion is very courageous. I think people spend a lot of energy and effort trying to hide them, and it's not because

The Feminine Sixth: Women for the Defense

they're strong. It's for a lot of other reasons. I think there are certain contexts, when you're standing with a client in front of a judge and he's getting a lengthy sentence that that does take a lot of strength to hold it together, and there's a professional purpose for that. But as far as feeling ashamed or embarrassed about feelings, I don't, really. I've cried in front of male coworkers. It's not like I — to me, it brings in the reality, which is this is a really sad situation, and I can feel that for a second and I can get back to work because I gave myself that time."

"What about expressing the 'hard' emotions, like anger? Can we talk about that a little bit? Expressing anger or getting loud or going hard after a witness on cross. These are all considered very masculine things," I respond, prompting Amanda to delve deeper into these issues.

"I think there's a lot of dynamics at play there too, because if you're black and you get angry, you're going to get a different reaction, too, from coworkers or from judges, juries even. As a woman, it's kind of like women aren't supposed to be that loud; women are supposed to be more patient. I think it's probably a little different now. As a woman at least, I feel I have support to be loud and be angry when it makes sense. Especially as a white woman I think I have that privilege. Getting loud with a witness on cross or getting angry with a witness on cross, I think, I'm sure there are some men on a jury that would dislike that. But I think from other professionals in the field that seems like something they would support," Amanda says.

"Well you are right about the 'it's okay if you're white' part of things," says Lisa. "But I think its other women that don't like you to 'overstep.' At least that has been my experience when I have taken on something tough."

"Lisa?" says Juanita, "Would you mind if I jumped in?"

Lisa smiles, looks at the audience, and says, "See? That's one way we are different. She *asked* before jumping in!" There are nods and some light laughter in the audience. "Sure, Juanita."

"I was thinking about anger, and how it can motivate, and get really good work going. When I was in the federal defender's office, my boss Gene Iredale brought a writ to unhandcuff prisoners who were charged with entering the country illegally. They would be brought into the courtroom in chains, chained together, charged with coming into this country illegally. What do you need to chain them together for? What are they going to do, run? They came here. They're not going to run away. That's why they're here, for God's sake, was to try to be here and not run back to Mexico. Anyway his motion was granted."

"But there was one particular magistrate that was really bad about it, and so since he could not chain them anymore, at least not in the courtroom, he found another means to humiliate and punish them. At that time your client could plead guilty to a misdemeanor, but that one particular magistrate, if they pled guilty to illegal entry in his courtroom, if he sentenced them — the maximum was six months. If he sentenced them to six months, they would get time off and they would do three and a half of the six, I think, or they would get good time. But you had to have a six-month sentence to qualify for good time. So he would sentence them to 179 days."

"To avoid them getting any good time?" I ask, incredulous.

Juanita nods, "So they wouldn't get any good time. And so we stopped entering pleas in front of him. We took everybody upstairs to the federal district court, before we would plead

The Feminine Sixth: Women for the Defense

them to the misdemeanor illegal entry. And the district court judges were furious. They're like, 'I have enough on my docket. What the hell am I doing taking up every Monday morning doing illegal entry pleas?' And we said, 'Well, talk to Magistrate Judge McCue. We are not going to enter a plea in front of him until he stops doing 179-day sentences.' And apparently they must have talked to him because he stopped. Oh, he was a total bigot, and I have no problem saying his name in front of everyone. A total bigot. He would say shit. He would take the bench and he would say, 'Oh, good morning, muchachos....' first of all, calling them 'boys,' right?"

"Seriously?" I ask.

"Seriously. 'Muchachos' means 'boys,'" Juanita responds. "And they weren't boys. 'Good morning, muchachos. So are you all from Tijuana?' Of course, he would say it as 'Tia Juana' because that's how Anglos say it. There is no 'a.' 'Tia Juana' means 'Aunt Juana.' 'Tijuana' is T-i-j-u. There is no extra 'a.' It makes me crazy. There's people in California who also can't even spell my first name. Anyway, he says to them, 'Are you all from 'Tia Juana?'' And of course, they're terrified. They don't know what to do so they're all nodding, 'Yes.' And then he would go, 'Oh, well, which one of you turned out the lights?' This is a running joke. Tijuana was now empty because there were so many of them in the box. He enjoyed screwing with these poor people, truly screwing with them. And it made me sick to my stomach to watch and to think that this is going on in our country and I didn't know about it. Nobody knew about it. You would have to come to court in San Diego to see it."

"Hmm," I respond. "So it made you angry?"

"Really angry." I could see her anger, right there. The cheery advocate was gone and the extremely tough one had taken her place. "So when you would get angry in court what would you do with that emotion?" I ask.

"I would channel it because obviously you are not there for yourself, you are there for your client. So you don't have a right to advance your agenda; you are advancing your client's agenda. So if it benefits your client to display emotion with the judge, you will display emotion with the judge. If it's not going to benefit your client, well, you will not. You will turn it in and do something positive with it. And so it just made me just want to be the best that I could. It made me try even harder to make sure that whatever little power I could take away from these judges, then I was going to do it. Does that make sense?"

"Yeah, it makes sense to me," I say. "One of the startling experiences I had was that displaying anger in the right circumstance could give you a lot of power, and it was something I was socialized not to do. Nice girls don't get angry in public. They don't get angry at all, but certainly not in public. The first time I got angry in court it just backed everyone down. I was like, 'Hmm. This is interesting.'" I looked around at the panel. "Anyone else want to weigh in about emotions in our work?" I ask.

"Well," says Huma, "Part of the challenge is figuring out what to do with your own anger. I mean, some days I've thought, I'm here for a reason, everything is working out great, this is exactly what I'm meant to do. It happens a lot after — I don't even want to say necessarily — 'wins' in court because that's so easy. Oddly enough, it happens sometimes after I get smacked in court, after my motion is completely denied and the judge disagrees with everything I say or after I get

The Feminine Sixth: Women for the Defense

reamed out on something. For example, a judge was really hoping to go to trial today and we're not ready and I have to explain why not, and I get reamed and I survive." Huma laughs and shrugs. I can see nodding on the panel, and some in the audience too. "Usually the moments where I feel like I'm really doing what I'm supposed to be doing, what I was called to do, are the moments where I get smacked and I feel my own resilience," she continues.

"Can you give me an example?" I ask.

"Sure. Like when a motion that I worked really hard on that I believe in, like a motion to suppress. I put in the arguments, I did the case law, I found some great cases, but the judge just didn't agree with me. But in the ruling, he said something or I said something, or both, that made it a good issue either for trial or for appeal. So even though I lost, there's a bit of a win there. And I think it's those qualified wins or qualified losses, I guess, that really, really pull me through, where I can see, yeah, I lost at this level, but if I think about it from another level, there's something there. So one thing that criminal defense has really taught me is to think everything through on multiple, multiple levels. It's never just what you see in front of you. You have to be way more creative than that. But sometimes after I have a tough day — oh, my favorite is, me and my best friend, we can be a bit crude, and we let off steam that way. Like he'll text me one day after he's had a rough morning in court and he'll be, like, 'Totally got moon pounded in Will County.'"

"Moon pounded?" I ask.

"Moon pounded," she repeats. There is laughter in the audience, but not so much on the panel. Some of them look nonplussed, too.

"Would you care to explain what that means?"

Huma sighs — it sounds remarkably like the sigh my son and daughter would utter at me during their teenage years. "It refers to anal sex," she says. Is she blushing? "It's something we say just among ourselves, just attorney solidarity, I guess, where I'm the one he vents to when he totally just got slammed by the judge. But the joke is we always do that after we're done, and the idea is that, yeah, we totally got reamed, but it's fine; we're moving on with our day. So there have been so many days where I went into court just dreading it, every single footstep towards that room, dreading it, because I knew that I was going to get yelled at, I knew I was not heading into a good situation, and the client was going to throttle me, the judge was going to throttle me."

"So I stepped up and everything went fine because I was able to control it. I would react to a judge's question or whatever, that smoothed the situation over, that made it okay. So those are definitely the moments where I really feel like I'm doing what I'm supposed to — when I can walk into something dreading it or being fearful and then coming out and thinking that that went fine."

"I remember feeling very alone," I say. "There was no one for me to talk to, I mean, when I started out. There just was no one."

Amanda nods. So do others on the panel.

"You have to understand," I continue, "that when I started defense work, there were hardly any other women, and we felt, or at least those few I talked to about this felt like we had to show how tough we were." I shake my head ruefully.

The Feminine Sixth: Women for the Defense

"I have a very strong memory of having no one to turn to with one case. It's one I talk about in my memoir, <u>Angel of Death Row: My Life As A Death Penalty Defense Lawyer</u>, where I talk about this battered woman I represented and how she showed me late in my representation of her where he had been putting cigarettes out on her chest." I take a deep breath. "I felt dizzy. I felt like I was going to faint or throw up, or both, and then I felt like I had to tamp it down."

Amanda says, "You had nowhere to go with that."

"No. Nowhere. It's one of the worst things I've ever seen in my life. I had to learn where emotion goes in this work. For example, sometimes you begin doing jury selection and a potential juror will say, 'Well, this is a robbery and I was robbed and I don't know if I can handle it,' you know, that kind of thing. And the judge will say something like — often — 'Can you put aside those feelings?' I'm thinking, 'Put them where? Is there a feeling bag that you dump them in as you go into the jury room and then pick them back up when you leave?' I mean, what do you do with them?"

Cyndy Short laughs. "I have never had a 'feeling bag' either!"

"And pretending that they don't exist doesn't help. You can't get so mired in feelings that you can't *see* either, and a lot of women talk about this balance issue, pretending not to feel anything. I don't know if this makes sense," I continue.

"Yeah, I think you are," says Amanda. "I think it's really common. I think sometimes it's helpful just to say out loud to someone else, with no response expected, 'I feel heartbroken about this; I need to tell you about this; I need to go somewhere with this.' It doesn't mean either of you is going to do anything about it. You might or you might not. But just having someone listen to you deeply and genuinely is so important — it's what we give our clients all the time — or at least we should — if you think about it."

"There is a whole other side to the emotions in our work too," says Huma. "The client never has one problem, the case. There are always a dozen other problems that really don't have much to do with the case, but kind of do, and you have to be aware of all of it. You have to be aware of what the client is going through in their life. You have to have a good sense or be able to get a good sense real quick of the prosecutor, what they're going through in their life, how they're approaching a case, because a lot of the times I've had a prosecutor who was fantastic on gun cases and drug cases but absolutely hated sex cases. Awareness of that would help. I learned fairly quickly — well, it took me a little bit of time to learn, let's put it that way, but I got a real good sense of how much you have to keep in your head at one time about all your cases that might not have much to do with the case at all."

"Well, you represent a person," says Cynthia Stewart. "They come with their baggage."

Huma nods. "Yup. And you're dealing with an opposing counsel who has stuff and you're dealing with a judge who has stuff. There's stuff in your office, there's stuff in your own life."

I break in. "We are going to talk about the 'stuff' in our lives too, but I am wondering if anyone from the audience has any questions?" There is a shuffling around and I see several people move to the two aisles where there are microphones. I find myself pleased that the questioners seem to be diverse in terms of gender, which is something I worried about when putting together the panel.

The Feminine Sixth: Women for the Defense

Another member of the audience steps up. She is wearing a flowy skirt and embroidered blouse, and outsized round glasses.

"I am wondering about secondary trauma here," she began. "As a number of you have shared how you do not wall off your emotions from your work, what do you do in terms of your own self-preservation and rejuvenation after pouring so much of yourself into your cases?" She pauses a minute, "I am not meaning to say you should wall off your feelings, but if you don't, how do you stay sane?"

"Well, to use a 'legal term,'" I begin, "you are assuming a fact not in evidence." My fellow panelists laugh and there is a smattering of laughter in the audience too — probably lawyers. "What I mean is maybe we aren't as sane as we look," I add.

"Now that is the truth," says Cynthia Roseberry, smiling impishly. "I think that it is really hard to be open and let yourself — and the jury — feel with you. I remember in a potential death case how strongly I felt — perhaps you can imagine the enormity of that burden?" She asks rhetorically. The room is very, very still. "While we were investigating his case, we went to see his school, and I remember crying because his school was so poor, he didn't have a chance. And I remember thinking that somewhere in the world somebody has a 14-carat gold toilet seat, and here they don't have enough books in the classroom, you know? Anyway, the Department of Justice decided not to seek the death penalty and once it went to a life case, I tried it as a life case, and he was convicted and he got life in prison. I remember speaking with the prosecutor later, saying, 'Listen, let's continue to work on this.' And she said, 'Yes. Once the victim is okay, the victim's family, we'll continue to work on this.' And for years

I continued to contact her — she left the office — to see if we could somehow get him transferred to Jamaica to serve his time. But the U.S. doesn't have a treaty with Jamaica, so we couldn't do that. I wrote to him and he's written to me. And when I took over the Clemency Project, I looked to see if somehow we could get him clemency. And the last time I wrote to him, I said, 'I want you to know I continue to work for your freedom; I can't let this go.' And he said to me, 'I'm okay. You don't need to worry about me anymore.' And he went to prison at 25, and he didn't kill anybody." Cynthia is crying. She sniffs "and he's going to spend the rest of his life in prison. That will always stay with me."

"I'm so sorry," I interject. Cynthia is shaking. "Are you okay?"

"Yeah, I'm okay," she says nodding as she spoke.

"Sometimes I find that when a client gets worried about how you feel, it feels like even more of a burden, if that makes sense. I mean, it's a positive thing, I guess, but it's. . ." I continue, and then stop.

Cynthia says, "Sure, because what I left out is once the verdict was rendered, you know, you go back into the little antechamber and they place him in the cell. So I can remember going back. And once they closed the cell, I grabbed the bars and I fell to my knees and I sobbed. And he reached his hand between the bars, patted me on the back, and said, 'It's okay.' He did that for me." Her tears are audible.

Cyndy Short walks over to Cynthia, and puts a steadying hand on her shoulder.

The Feminine Sixth: Women for the Defense

I look around the audience. No one has come to the microphone, so I turn to the panelists and ask them, "How do you get a sense of what level of emotional engagement is going to most positively affect both your relationship with your client and your representation of that client?"

Crystal Marchigiani responds, "You know, I feel that things have changed; maybe that's why I have retired. I've been both young and old in this business, but I've always been female and I've always been white, so it isn't that that's changed. It's a demand mentality that I think really does make it hard to feel the connection, the emotional connection, that was always the reason that I was pulled into the work and was always the thing that sustained me even in the bad cases, you know, even in the 'Oh, my God, are you going down' cases, I cared about the client. I was able to care about the client. I didn't feel like the client was making demands on me. Maybe here's the difference: I felt like the client and I were in it together and maybe against all odds. Certainly those are most of your cases. You and I are in this against all odds, but it's you and me. That's important to both of you. I am not sure that is what is happening anymore. Or maybe, not happening for me anymore."

"Has anyone had a client who, well, turned on her?" I ask.

Cynthia speaks up. "Oh, I had a client. So that would be Batman."

"Seriously? Batman?" asks Juanita.

Cynthia nods. "Yup. Batman. His name was Batman because he used a baseball bat to discipline the nine-year-old and ten-year-old girls he pimped." The audience reacts with what you might expect, I see folks murmuring among themselves.

"Oh, good God. Nine and ten years old?" says Cynthia Stewart.

"Nine and ten years old," Cynthia responds. "And, of course, he wasn't happy to be appointed a woman lawyer. I have a court drawing of Batman in the courtroom because he's so often complained about me, the court artist decided to draw Batman complaining about me. And he kept telling the judge, 'I don't want this woman. She's a woman, and I don't want this lawyer.'"

"He couldn't accept me as a woman, but he taught me more than any other client, though. He said horrible things to me. I went and bought him clothes with my own money, and he said, 'I don't wear clothes like that. I won't wear that.' But he taught me that the feelings that I have for a client don't have to be requited in order for me to care about their defense, right? So what I had to cling to was my belief that unless all of us get it, none of us get the protection of the Constitution, right? So he helped me realize my commitment. He helped me walk the talk I've been talking for so long, right: that the Constitution is for everyone, and the moment we choose that some get the benefit of it and that others don't, we all lose, and the least among us won't ever get it. I had always said that and believed that, but he really taught me how to operate in a place where that belief is what undergirded my ability to defend him more than my feelings for him as a client."

A middle aged slender white man steps to the microphone. He looks like he got dressed in order to try to look like a professor. Were those elbow patches on his jacket? "Sir?" I ask. "You had a question?"

He clears his throat; he sounds like he had a cold or maybe allergies. "Can any of you talk about how you managed to represent someone who was accused of committing a crime

The Feminine Sixth: Women for the Defense

that you yourself, or a friend, family, or coworker, have been the victim of? Something that hit close to home?"

Cynthia Stewart speaks up. "I think it's hard when you feel like you're seen as being on 'the wrong side,' whether or not you have been a victim yourself. Sex assault cases in Mississippi are tough because we have horrible statutory rape laws. It's based on there being 36 months' difference in age. It's a little more complicated than that. But, for example, that would include a lot of what went on in my high school because freshman girls just love to be asked out by the senior boys. Some of those senior boys are 18 and there's more than 36 months' difference so technically they're in violation of the law — and it's a strict liability crime if they have proof. Technically these days, that would be a violation of that statute."

"I had a case that I worked on with a lawyer who is up in Canton, an 18-year-old boy, not much bigger than me, little fine, blond hair and still had the bowl cut, still watched SpongeBob SquarePants, and he had sex. Proof couldn't be overcome, the judge wouldn't let us get in our questions from what she had posted on Facebook about her — she had one picture of herself not completely, but fairly, naked, and she had used some kind of stamp to do fake tattoos all over her body. She was tall and lanky, but she would be easy to dress up to look much younger than she typically did, and we were precluded from getting out the fact that she runs around in a little teeny bikini all over the neighborhood — not that I think that justifies it — but it was consensual. I took the case and tried talking it out with everybody I knew, including the people who would tend to be sympathetic. We were considering trying to get jury nullification, which would have been the only way to win that, but I couldn't get it past anybody. You just are representing the 'wrong' person, and as a mom I don't want rapists running around, but I also think we can go too far. I hate that not only as a lawyer; I hate that as a mother. If I go on a sex registration site, I want to know who is a predator. I don't give a rat's ass about an 18-year-old who had sex, consensual sex, with a 15-year-old that was not — there was no force or, you know, authority by the teacher or something like that. All they have done is clutter it up so that it becomes sort of meaningless, at least in Mississippi." Cynthia Stewart is shaking her head.

"I had a close relative who was raped," I say. "Every woman's nightmare. She was living in a ground floor apartment, and woke up to find the rapist on top of her with a knife." I swallow. "I was scheduled to start a trial the next day — it had been a Saturday night/Sunday morning. So I cancelled everything and flew out to where she was to help. We stayed in a hotel and before returning to her apartment, we bought a whole new bed. It was so awful. Anyway, a day or two after I got there, I went with her to the police station for a follow up interview. It turned out that this was a serial rapist, and she was his twentieth victim or something. I brought a book with me so I could sit in the lobby while they talked to her. The police officer must have asked her if she had someone with her, and what I did for a living, because the officer came out with that walk." I turn to the other panelists. "You know the 'cock first' cop walk?" I get nods. "And he says to me that the guy was probably one of my clients that I had gotten out on a technicality. His language was less polite than that." I could hear some gasps in the audience.

"Uh oh," says Lisa Wayne. "He shouldn't have done that." She smiles ruefully.

"No he shouldn't have," I respond. "I asked him, loudly so the whole station could hear, if he was willing to take off his badge, leave his gun, and come outside and say that shit to me. I was so mad, and hurt, and jumbled up. I think I would have taken a swing at him, but he kind of slinked off. My relative came out after that to go home and looked between us, she could see something had happened. She asked me what and I mumbled nothing, and we got out of there."

Lisa says, "I hate that. It's like you think murder is a good idea if you defend someone charged with it." All of the panelists are nodding.

I tell the audience to take a short break, that we are coming back to speak directly about gender — and race — in our work.

CHAPTER THREE:
WOMAN IN A WHITE MAN'S WORLD

"We are now going to talk specifically about what it means to be a woman doing this work, in a man's world. Specifically, in a white man's world," I begin. "These are touchy subjects, I know, but it's part of the reason you all are here, right?" I ask the audience. I see some nods, and some head shakes and some shifting in chairs. I can't see faces that well, but I bet there is some eye rolling going on.

"So I want to start out asking each of our panelists to talk about how gender and race have affected them in the practice of law, especially as criminal defense lawyers. I know that it is hard to have a real conversation about these divisive issues, especially after the 2016 U.S. presidential election. Personally, I think I am suffering from PTSD since that election." I get some laughter then. "I am going to go in the opposite order starting with the end of the alphabet, so that would be you, Lisa Wayne." Lisa walks to the podium. She walks like a dancer.

"Let me start with high school, I went to a huge public high school where there was a lot of racism. The television miniseries 'Roots' had come out when I was a junior, I think. I graduated from high school in, I think, 1977. I went to a predominantly white high school. Black kids were very segregated. They were the kids who were bussed in. I wasn't part of that group because I was in my neighborhood, so I was part of the kids

The Feminine Sixth: Women for the Defense

who were white. But I really wasn't, as I learned when 'Roots' was released. I just remember when 'Roots' came out and kids talking about it and ridiculing it and really making fun of it."

"Ridiculing it?" I ask, surprised.

"Yes. And calling me 'Kunta Kinte,' I mean, really cruel things in hindsight. And I would brush it off. I loved 'Roots.' 'Roots' had a huge impact on me as a black kid watching it, right, on television, and going, wow, look at this history that nobody talks to you about. I had learned it, of course, in the home, and it had a great impact on me. But I went to a very racist high school. Let me give you an example. I dated a white guy who was on the football team. I dated him for a couple of years in high school. There was a lot of talk behind my back and people telling him, you know, 'how he could be dating me.' Then I learned he passed me off with his family as being Hawaiian."

"Really? Oh wow," says Cynthia Roseberry.

"Yeah. Absolutely. Absolutely," says Lisa.

"Can I take a pause for a moment and ask you: You have a mixed-race background, correct?" I ask.

"Absolutely."

"Would you mind describing that and maybe talking a little bit about how that has affected you?"

Lisa takes a breath. "I think it had a great impact on me becoming a defense lawyer coming from a mixed background. When I was growing up, I was black. I was never anything else — my parents, we didn't have a discussion about 'You can be other things' or 'You have this in your background.' You were black. My parents recognized, particularly in their growing up, if you had any black in you, you're black, you're perceived by others as black, and that's who you are. The problem was I had an absence of a black community in my life. So all that was good to understand, but I only had white friends and I grew up around whites. So I didn't have that community of blacks who looked like me, who came from mixed backgrounds, and who had that same experience. It's interesting."

"When I graduated from high school, my parents really made a push for me to go to Spelman College, a historically black liberal arts college for women in Atlanta, Georgia. I rejected that totally. I was not going to go to a black school. In hindsight, I get what was going on. They thought that would give me this feeling and sense of belonging that I hadn't really had, but there was no way that was going to happen with me. I said, 'No, I'm not going to Spelman. What are you talking about?'"

"My father's father is white, his mother is black and Indian, we think. His mother died when he was a kid, and he never knew his father, but we really don't know the story there. I'm sure there are a lot of reasons for that. My dad doesn't really care to know, he doesn't want to know who his father was, and he's very clear about that. His grandmother was a schoolteacher on the black side of town in Mississippi, so she raised him until he was about seven, eight years old. There are the stories that he remembers that because he looked white — he's very fair-skinned — she would pass him off for white to be able to sit on the front of the bus, to be able to get educated at the Catholic schools. So the nuns were great and the Catholic schools and the Catholic religion was very good about educating blacks in the South, but you had to pass a certain lighted-skinned, look-more-white test. So the

The Feminine Sixth: Women for the Defense

dark black kids were not getting educated. It was the kids who looked more white."

"Good heavens," I respond. "To what degree do you think that your gender has affected you, positively or negatively, as well as race?"

"You know, that's interesting, Andrea, in terms of my gender because being black — and you'll hear this from a lot of women of color — my gender was not something that I was focused on in my career, or in my life, frankly, because being black had much more of a focus for me about how I was treated and the way I navigated the world. My gender was kind of something that I sidelined, frankly. It was not the most important point to me. I look back at it and I think, was I treated differently? Was I treated more favorably?"

"I think being a black woman, being a woman of color, is one of the hardest gigs going, frankly, even today. I think I would be less than truthful to not admit that the way that I look probably was beneficial to me. I don't like to think of it that way. I remember coming back to the public defender's office after a string of wins on really hard cases, really ugly cases that people would say, 'You can't win those. If you go to trial, you can't win those.' Some of the male lawyers in the office were saying, 'It's because of the way you look, not because you're a good lawyer, but because of the way you look.' I go, 'Really? You think people are walking murderers and people who are accused of rapes because of the way I look? I mean, give me a break.' So it was a disadvantage to some extent, but it's an advantage. I mean, the way you look is an advantage in the world. So I'm sure that I got treated by my male colleagues and maybe my bosses in a different way because they thought I was attractive. I never had a relationship with a boss or someone in a senior position. I never used my sex for ever getting those kind of benefits from higher-ups. I certainly dated my share of colleagues, but who didn't? We're incestuous, we're an incestuous group, because who else can stand us except us? Nobody. So gender may have played a role in terms of maybe giving me some breaks."

"If I could interrupt one second. When men would say, 'You got this because of your looks,' did you feel like what they were really doing was minimizing your accomplishment?" I ask.

"Absolutely."

"And do you think that was race or gender or both?" I glance at the other panelists. They are hanging on her every word.

"I think in the public defender's office it was more gender because we had a pretty good, diverse office when I started. Not to say that you can't be of color and still have your stereotypes about people in your own race or those things. I don't know. That's a complicated question."

"I know that there were a lot of women. David Vela, who was the head of the office, hired a lot of us and we were a tough group of women, and we were diverse, from Cuban to white to — I was the only black woman that was in my group. There were a couple black women ahead of me that didn't stay, but then I was the only woman in the whole system for many, many years. But we hung tough together. We're still very close friends. They're some of my best friends. They called us 'The Committee,' the men did, because they were very threatened by us and that was their way of hiding or excusing their discomfort. So it's a joke to this day, 'The Committee,'" she chuckles.

The Feminine Sixth: Women for the Defense

"It's a little bit nicer than what we called us, the women that were in my office — 'The Coven,'" I reply.

"It's that same thing. And they used to say that about SunWolf, who is now a professor at Santa Clara and was a legendary public defender. They would say that about her because she was extraordinary and they were very intimidated by it. A lot of my black lawyer friends who talk about this, the woman issue, and a lot of times we'll be in a group talking about, you know, whiny white women, they don't get it. They don't get how easy it is for them. And the reality is that white women took more advantage of affirmative action than any other group for schools. That's factually, statistically true. You go to law schools and, I mean, you see that, okay? So a lot of women of color really kind of resent that whole deal. I know. It's interesting. That's a book in and of itself. So we talk about it amongst ourselves. We would never talk about it in public, I don't think." She pauses, "Until now I guess."

"That's very interesting. It also is reflected in the split in the women's movement, the feeling that women of color were not really being considered by the leadership," I reply.

"Right. Right. And how hard it is to be black. Statistically, we get the worst car deals, we get the worst mortgage rates, I mean, all of these things that are always on your back, being black first. It was when that whole celebrity thing came but, what's her face was talking about equal pay, the movie star and white women aren't getting paid the same as other male movie stars, and a lot of women of color were, like, 'Are you kidding me?' Do you know how much we make compared to the average white movie star? That's how a lot of people feel. That's not my focus. I get it."

"Do you have an example of a time when your gender was a salient factor in court?" I ask Lisa.

"I do. The chief judge, the first day that I appeared in front of him, Judge Tracey, he said to me, as I was standing up there with my black client, the mother — no, there was no mother — standing up there with the black client, says to me, 'Excuse me, but parents aren't allowed to stand up near the lectern. Where is the lawyer?' because he didn't know me and I hadn't had a chance to introduce myself. I said, 'I am the lawyer, Judge,' and he was mortified. But I didn't call him out; I didn't do anything, and he, I think, to his dying day appreciated that. And from that point on, he was always wonderful to me. But they had never seen someone like me before."

"I can't say if I got pigeonholed because it was in the public defender's office, and there was supposedly a random assignment system. I never even thought about that then. In private practice, absolutely I recognize that I get hired because I'm a woman, and I do think it's true: We are better at some cases, especially sexual assault cases perhaps because they are very difficult in terms of some of the very complicated issues that may go along with them — like the boundary issues. That's why you want women jurors on the cases, frankly. We are much more open to explanations, whereas men are not."

"Now, that's not all men and that's not all women. You can't generalize. I've seen some men do some incredible cross-examinations on alleged sex assault victims with children and grown women, so it can go both ways. But I think that there is something that we may bring to the table, and I think that's okay, because men may bring to the table a different element on pornography cases — I don't know — that are more understanding than we are. I don't know. So I don't shy away from the fact that maybe I'm much more comfortable

The Feminine Sixth: Women for the Defense

talking about vaginas than men are, you know, or intercourse or fellatio or having the whole '50 Shades of Grey' kind of sex. I mean, maybe we are more comfortable with it. I think I'm probably very comfortable with my sexuality, and that has a lot more to do with it, and being able to talk about those things because I know a lot of women who won't touch these cases, who can't deal with them, who don't want to deal with them. So I don't know."

"And the appearance in the courtroom? I think this goes both ways these days, because jurors are very savvy, and a lot of that has to do with social media and television. You have jurors that say, you know, 'I can't help but think, Ms. Wayne, that he probably hired you because you're a woman and you seem very likable.' I've had lots of jurors say that."

"How do you respond?" asks Huma.

Lisa looks at Huma, "Well, I would respond to the juror like this. 'That's a very interesting thing that you brought to our attention, and I'm wondering why you're thinking about that.' Of course, I'm not going to change your mind about it, but I wonder how many others of you think the same way? Because if you do, that gives me information, right, that you may not be a good juror. So tell me about that. So I'm perfectly fine with that. I think that's probably true, but the same goes if you're a black lawyer and you've got a black client. Did they hire you because you're black? A lot of black clients say, 'It's a disservice to me to have a black lawyer.' They don't want you. And in my experience Latin clients are the most difficult. Now I'm finding that Asian clients fall right up there."

Juanita asks, "Why? I mean Latino clients in particular? Are there others that you find problematic?"

Lisa thinks for a moment. "Look, I know I am painting with a broad brush here, but other women of color, that's a tough one too. Maybe it's because of the stereotype that the one that has the most power in the courtroom is a white guy, so naturally that's who I want defending me. A woman of color is marginalized in society, so why shouldn't she be in the courtroom? And the jurors feel the same way about them. So they have got enough to overcome. They don't need you on the case."

"Boy, it's complicated," I comment.

"It's very complicated. And it's interesting because most of my clients in private practice are white, white people who have money who don't even think twice about having me because they want the best lawyer. I know. It's very interesting to me. Another thing that is interesting regarding gender though is that I keep thinking, people are going to start saying what they said about a well-known woman defender when she left. I would hear people say, 'God, she's getting older; is she in menopause, because she seems like she's angry all the time.' And I was like, oh, my God, they're going to start saying, 'God, Lisa seems like she's angry all the time; is she in menopause?'" Lisa laughs, and so do many of the panelists. Not the younger ones, though I notice.

"Well, do you think that's something they would say about a woman but not a guy who is angry all the time?" Amanda asks Lisa.

"I think so, yes. That's right. I know that. So you do start thinking that, as I'm fanning myself." Now there is more widespread laughter. "But as I get older, I've become an angrier black woman. I've become angry about being black, I've become angry about what's happening to the clients. I have this angst that I just didn't have on the surface all the time when I was younger. So that part, you go, 'Okay,' you don't want that to interfere with your representation, and maybe that's telling you it's time that you've got to change it up. I don't get to do anything until Dylan is out of college, so I've got to get my son out of college. So retirement, I just want to have acknowledgment of my shortcomings of when it's a good time to go. What's interesting is if you go around courtrooms all over this country on criminal cases, you see older white guys, I mean, old guys, doing criminal practice, right? And they're kind of the dignified old white criminal lawyer. You don't see older women doing this practice in the courtroom. That's part of why the issue of race is so complicated and so divisive and hurtful and emotional. There's just so many levels to it."

"Yeah. There really are," I say.

"Next up is Cynthia Stewart. Cynthia, I have to say that I have some predisposition about racial issues in the south, especially Mississippi, but I am not sure how accurate they are or the role that sexism might play for a woman criminal defense lawyer there."

"Well," she begins, deliberately drawing out the southern drawl, "That's true. In some ways, it can be easier since things are more on the table. When I was growing up, you sent your child to private school, or you did if you were white anyway. At that time, private schools were largely, not exclusively, but a couple that were little parochial schools, but that — segregation programs. When my parents moved to Madison County, they did enroll us all in the school that had grown up out there with segregation programs. Somewhere in the first quarter, I put my foot down and refused to go to school."

"How old were you when you did this?" I ask.

"Young. I'm trying to remember the exact sequence, but it was, I think, prior to high school. It just seemed flawed to me, and what little I saw in the few weeks I went only further cemented that. I can remember a coach who — it wasn't just black/white segregation, but the teaching in classes could be very derogatory about women and girls and what they could do and where they were going to end up. It just didn't sit well. It caused quite a family feud. Eventually my father backed me up. Back when I was — well, we grew up getting dropped off at the Presbyterian Church. You know, 'Do what I say, not what I do.' I remember being very affected by something I found kind of by accident in the school library — perhaps because nobody was paying attention — but it was a collection of underground newspaper articles, and it had a lot about feminism in there."

"Did anybody ever sort of actively say to you, 'You're too uppity. You need to be more girly?'" asks Cyndy Short.

"Oh, my mother did all the time. She wasn't overly fond of me and she didn't like my rebelliousness and did what she could to dampen my self-esteem and, in fact, damaged it for a period of years. But eventually I found it again."

"Back to my original observation, do you feel that your feminism looks different because of being from Mississippi?" I ask.

"Women aren't expected to act like men in order to be equal, would be my starting point. I don't wear suits anymore. I mean, I dress professionally, but I gave up dry cleaning as my contribution to a greener world. I was nicely dressed. Sometimes I had my cowboy boots on with my skirt. Southern women are — I didn't learn it very well; I didn't learn it until I was close to 30, but from a very young age, most southern women have a knack for dealing with men. It's something that you're just kind of taught. It's not necessarily a bad thing. Usually our toenails are painted and it's important that you look your best. What I've seen from lawyers, for example, coming down from the DA's, they wear the same suit as the men, and it looks terrible, you know, a boxy skirt. There's some it looks good on, but mostly it's not a very flattering item of clothing, for one. And part of it is that it is a fraternalistic society, and I don't mean 'sexist' by that, because it's not so much that — well, it's very hard to explain."

"There was an assistant DA who is retired now, and I could get better deals out of him than anybody else. I actually had a formula for it. It involved sitting there and listening to him talk about his 'old boy' stories for about an hour about when he used to be a criminal defense lawyer and practiced up in Northern Mississippi. We'd chat a bit about his daughter and what she was doing now, and we had got around to the case. I paid him a couple of compliments and asked him about his daughter, and increasingly we'd come to a resolution about the case. What was funny about it is I was sitting with a couple of his buddies, they'd got three of them who all moved down from Northern Mississippi to work in Hinds County at the same time. None of them were still there. I can't remember where we were, but we were sitting around and joking, and he says, 'Yeah, I'll tell you how Cynthia deals with Kessler,' and he sat down and described exactly what I did. 'She just goes in there and listens to his stories and flatters him a little bit.' I'm, like, 'What are you doing? Listening at the door?'" She chuckles deep in her throat.

"And do you feel like that's — some people would say that that's unfair or that's trading on — flirting, or whatever words you want to use," asks Amanda, looking a bit shocked. Well, not shocked, but disapproving maybe?

"Everybody in the South flirts," drawls Cynthia, her accent deliberately pronounced. "It works the other way, too. I've seen male lawyers flirt with assistant DAs. It's just kind of — culturally acceptable. It's just kind of a way of interacting. Like I said, I learned it late in life. It wasn't something I picked up growing up. I was a terrible tom boy, much more interested in running around and playing baseball with the boys and skinning my knees. I think we all use what we have. I'm not sure it's any different than the good old boys talking about the latest football game. It's the pre-talk before you get to figuring out the case."

"I am going to ask Christine Start to speak next."

"My identity as a woman and a Filipina plays a big part my life and that has a lot to do with just growing up with a lot of Filipinos. I can speak basic Tagalog. My parents worked a lot when I was younger, and I actually witnessed them go from not making very much money to being pretty well-off and having this nice two-story home, three-car garage. So my aunt and uncle (they're actually my grandparents' siblings), raised me as a child, so they spoke a lot of Tagalog. That's how I understand Tagalog. My siblings don't really speak it, so I think it was just kind of being around them. I was very ingrained with that culture. Every weekend, if not every day, I would be eating Filipino food. After school I would go to my grandparents' house every day, so I was just always around Filipinos. I think it's just part of my identity and who I identify with, and I think I clung more to that identity when I left, when I went to college, and law school, too."

"My culture is very conservative and my liberalism didn't really come out until I went to Cal and started exposing myself to just sitting in classes and listening and learning about how there's so much injustice in the world, and money and corporations dominate this world. It's so unfair. I didn't even know — I didn't face any racism or prejudices growing up in a city with a lot of Filipinos. I was very lucky in that way. And it wasn't until I got to Cal where I realized that I actually felt inferior to many, many people. I didn't have super rich friends. It was a whole new world for me, being exposed to people that I was just not used to being exposed to. So I just started opening my eyes and talking to people and seeing people. Let's see. Affirmative action was a big deal while I was at Cal. I didn't even know what that was until I got to college."

Christine looks over at the other panelists and kind of shrugs.

"When I started law school, more than half the school was still white. Even though we're a school that prides ourselves on diversity, I felt like an outcast. And I also did not feel smart next to these people. I did not talk like them. So when I actually was in this class and I saw people that I associated with that were more like me, I was, like, okay, but why is it we who struggle? I also recognized that I just wasn't good at taking tests, and 'we' had that in common. My LSAT score was not very good, and I took it a couple times. Who writes the test? Probably white people. I don't want to say it's a cultural thing, but just the way you associate words. Like, even me. My boyfriend makes fun of me. I say, 'Close the light,' all the time. It's 'Turn off the light.' But in Tagalog you say 'close,' so there are all these little things."

"I recognize there's a disadvantage when the majority of 'How to Graduate Law School' is written by white people and things of that nature. It's in your subconscious that that's happening. So how does it feel? It felt like this sucks; I have to work harder than I thought I did, which is fine, because to me college wasn't that hard. At Cal, I majored in political science and mass communications, and I definitely was one of those people that didn't study for the finals until the week of or the week before. So law school was just such a — it was me developing the habit and practice of really knowing how to study. I tended to just bond more with people that were like me more than anything. That saying, like, 'the struggle is real.' Well, with me, it is. It was real for me in law school."

"I thought I was going to get kicked out or I wasn't going to make it, because there were a good amount of people that didn't," Christine continues. I mean, it's what we're going through right now in terms of just bringing race to the forefront, right? We have this committee now that the public defenders in the Bay Area formed called Public Defenders for Racial Justice, and we talk about all kinds of things. One of the things that stands out to me is your book Andrea, actually. You mention at least twice about bringing up race in front of the jury, and we try and do that more and more, like, how can we incorporate race in our legal arguments? How can we incorporate just getting to know our clients as a person, human to human, and making that something we can showcase to the jury or to the judge? So we do trainings on how to do that, which is really, really cool. And the reason we're doing it is because it's a big issue now with all these black kids basically being murdered by police officers who are white."

"Are there different challenges regarding race for you as a Filipina? I mean different from the ones we usually think of like black, white, Latino?" I ask.

Christine nods, chewing on her bottom lip a bit. "Just growing up, you know, Filipinos tend to not like black people. Dark skin is not favored. The number one makeup product is skin bleach in the Philippines."

The Feminine Sixth: Women for the Defense

"God. That's so universal. And sad," says Cynthia Roseberry.

"It's ridiculous," Christine responds.

"So I want to ask you something, but it feels a bit odd, Christine," I start. "Can you talk a little bit about your gender, and the fact that you're very pretty and you're very small? Those are facts. How do you think that that has affected or not affected the work that you do?"

"Okay. I mean, it definitely makes — I think it's part of just who I am generally, of course, right? But in terms of how it affects me as a lawyer, I think I'm underestimated a lot, and people look at me and it takes some time, especially for my clients, it takes some time for them to decide whether or not I'm worthy and/or capable of really fighting for them, right? When they look at me, they don't see that. But when they hear me and I'm always on their side, it's not just my job, it's what I believe in, right? I think for the most part, the clients know I get it. They know I get it once they hear me articulate their case and once they know and believe that I'm on their side."

"Do clients ever talk to you about it directly? I mean do you get hit on? That used to happen to me, but, of course, I was one of, like, two women doing this work anywhere in the beginning of my career," I respond.

"I think I shut them down pretty quickly when they do. What they will do is they will hit on me, and I'll get that not just from my clients, but from other inmates, too, that happen to be at the jail there at the same time. They'll be, like, 'How do you be my lawyer? How do I get someone pretty like you?' I'll get that on the side while I'm talking to my client and I just kind of shut that out. A lot of the time it's not worth engaging in. But with my clients, I will have clients that will hit on me or will be, like, 'Oh, so are you married?' or 'How come you don't have a ring on your finger?' You know, sometimes they will be really nice to me and I know that it's because of how I look. But I — it's never — the way that I deal with it is I don't want to ruin our relationship or make them think I have something up my ass because I want to be friendly with them, because I want to work together and I want them to trust me and help them be open with me in terms of taking me seriously. The way that I get over it is I just say, 'Look, that's not what I'm here for. I can't stop you from looking at me, but I hope you're listening to me. And I'm just kind of hurt.' It makes them squirm. And usually they care about themselves, so they are going to listen. I don't really — I haven't had any encounters where I felt completely violated in that way with my clients. For the most part, we get along very well. I mean, if they hit on me, they hit on me. I just handle it."

"I would be interested to hear from any of you panelists a bit later about this issue, if you are willing?" I look at the panelists and can see them all remembering 'the time that...' Well I am remembering a few instances too. "Christine, how about with colleagues or other 'players' in the system?"

"With colleagues, I feel like — I think it's more in my head than it is in anyone else's head — but I feel like I have high expectations for myself, and sometimes I think, oh, are they looking down on me or do they think I'm not speaking up because I'm Asian or I'm small? But no one has outright — as a colleague, no one has ever outright made me feel that because I'm a woman, I can't do the job. I've never really felt that way with colleagues. I think any doubt I have with regard to whether I'm smart enough, what I'm learning is it's just coming from me and my instinct, my insecurities. With DAs, I think that they think that they can intimidate me, and so I'm very nice. When I'm in the courtroom, I like to try to develop collegial relationships with my colleagues because ultimately I think it will benefit my client if I need to deal and/or get what I want out of it. I don't know if it's because I'm a woman, I don't know if it's because I'm Filipino or Asian or because I'm, quote, unquote, pretty, or something that they think they can get away with more, but I won't let them get away with it if I can do something about it." Christine pauses and thinks for a moment.

"Once I was confronted with what I believed to be racism from a judge and I used my gender, I think, to my advantage with another judge. That one case I was telling you about with the kid where we had to get all these different departments together, well, he had been doing really well in the group home and he had a progress report, and he had come to court and the judge — you know, this boy had matured. He was 14 and now he's 15 and grew like — he had one of those growth spurts. He was looking taller. He didn't look as much like a kid anymore. When I met him, he was a kid. Now he was becoming a teenager. He walked out of the courtroom, my client, with his mom, the mom was there even with him in this group home, and I heard the judge mumble under his breath — not even under his breath, just outright to the clerk, 'Now he has the size to back up his next robbery.'"

"Seriously?" I say.

"Seriously. I don't think he would have said that if the child was white. And I don't know if the judge saw me, because I was crouched down gathering my stuff to leave, and I was so in shock by what he said, and to him it was, like, so funny, you know? I didn't know what to do. I left the courtroom, but I made a loud noise as I walked out the door so he knew I was there and I heard him say it, because I don't think he realized I was in the courtroom when I heard it. And I didn't know what to do, but I was so pissed. I talked to my colleagues in the office, whoever was there. And my boss said, 'Why don't you just go talk to him about it? Before we turn it into a big deal, you should just talk to him and tell him where you're coming from and why that's affected you and why it's wrong.' And I was, like, 'Yeah, you're right. I need to do something. It's not okay.' And I was thinking long-term that this is my judge and I can't — I still have to have a relationship with him, and he did what was right in that case in terms of the progress report and things like that."

"So the next morning I approached him and I asked if we could have an in-chambers discussion. I just explained to him what I was feeling, and my emotions really came out and I ended up, like, tearing up, and I was free to say that I worked so hard on this case, and he's improved. The last thing I or anyone could ever want is for him to go out there and not do — or, I mean, to do something wrong, to do something that could back-check him. And I said that he's got so much potential. I just explained it to him. I don't know if the crying really hit him; he's not an emotional kind of judge. He has no emotion, actually. People say he has a reputation for not caring and not caring to the point that it disadvantages them. He used to be a DA. Again, he likes to send people to jail and prison. But I ended up opening him up, and then he started telling me about his son and his kids and that one of his kids is autistic and how his wife almost divorced him because of something he said about, I think, the kid, and just kind of really opened up to me. I know I recognized he's human just like my clients are human, and you say that things are deplorable and despicable. For him, it's humor, you know, and for me, it's personal, and for my client it's personal. I was, like, 'That was really, really disrespectful and wrong for you to say.' He offered to get off the case, and it was a really powerful moment for me."

The Feminine Sixth: Women for the Defense

"Wow," says Cyndy Short. "That took courage, to let him see you like that."

I nod. "Cyndy, that is a nice transition — it's your turn," I tell her with a grin. "To what degree do you feel like being a woman and a criminal defense attorney has either mattered or not mattered or been good or been bad or both?"

"Well, it was a man's world. Mostly white men too. When I joined the public defender's office I think, particularly when I was in the trial office, I — because I was in the trial office and then I went and was in the conflicts office, which was a very small office; there were only three women and an investigator. I was never a shrinking violet. I always had kind of a command about what I wanted to do, and I never seemed to have a problem with the judges in terms of them demeaning me or acting like I was different than the guys. And I prided myself, I think, on being a trial lawyer, I was going into it as being more accepted as one of them, truthfully. It's not to the sense that I — I wasn't like that woman at the labor law firm where I started who felt so threatened by me, and, as a result of that, she was so rejecting of me. I never experienced that with the other women. I've always been very collegial, you know, very team-building. You can bring anyone into the office with any kind of pedigree and any kind of experience, and I'm ready to take them on as part of my community and part of my — what is that term? That it takes a village? — part of my village to do what I have to do. I've always been in a — in our trial office, if you went to trial, you went to trial with two lawyers always."

"That was the same in the Chicago public defender's office," I respond. "Let me ask you this, what would you say to a young woman contemplating becoming a criminal defense attorney?"

"How would I do that? Hmmm. I would warn her first that there's been for me over the course of the last decade or maybe 15 years, a tremendous sadness in the sense that when I first walked into a courtroom, I believed in it being a solemn place where justice occurred, where people were treated fairly, where outcomes were based upon the truth, and I honestly believed that. And it really took a long time for me to not be that naive about the whole thing. There's a certain safety in that place, and I almost envied my brothers and sisters who lived in this make-believe world where they could believe that courts worked correctly and poor people were treated the same way as rich people and all of that business. So I think I would warn a new lawyer coming into this to be bolder, to have their eyes more, and to understand that the challenge is so significant and that they really are on the good side of this fight; it's not the prosecution."

"And why be a criminal defense lawyer? Because — I guess you look at this Black Lives Matter thing, it's — because of the people that we come into contact with, from my perspective, their lives matter, and there are very few people who speak for the poor in a way that can translate. Is that the right way to say it? There's so many people that are so damaged by our criminal justice system that we need good people to come in and be able to be brave enough to really fight, to really yell and scream when you really need to be yelling and screaming, when you are willing to say, regardless of whether you get the next case from that judge, that what's happening here is wrong. And it takes time and courage to be able to do that. And then you find yourself 15 years into your career and you didn't — you waited too long until you really realized it. And now that you've realized it and you're willing to seemingly break rules — I don't even think I'm breaking rules now. I think I'm just marching right up to the edge and hugging that line as close as I can, and I'm willing to do and say things and challenge those people that are in power. I guess that's a

The Feminine Sixth: Women for the Defense

large part of what keeps you going, because there aren't a lot of people that are doing this, you know? There's not a lot of people yelling loud enough. And a part of you says, 'The futility of it, what can one person really do?' And so I have to examine that tension that comes from just representing one person, versus trying to take on the system. I would like what I'm doing here to have a broader effect, but the fact of the matter is I'm responsible for this life right now, and I'm going to do everything I can to make a difference in this life."

"I know that this part of the program is running long," I say. "Do we need a break now?" I see some nods and people heading for the exits so I tell them ten minutes. I figure there might be some washroom needs for the panelists as well. "Cynthia," I say to Cynthia Roseberry as she gets up to make use of the facilities. How did she manage those heels? "You are next."

"I know," she says, grinning and walking off, gracefully.

After the audience settles back in, I turn to Cynthia Roseberry. "Cynthia, I am wondering if you could talk to us about some of your experiences. Have you ever felt that you were directly asked to do something — or not do it — because of your gender?"

"Oh yes," she says in her deliberate, musical, and cadenced tone. "I would always get called in by a male lawyer who had a rape case or something where a woman was needed in the case."

"Can you talk about that for a minute? I'm smiling because, of course, I know exactly what you're talking about." I look at the other panelists who are nodding and smiling too. The room goes absolutely silent and all eyes are on Cynthia Roseberry.

"I can remember one rape client in particular who didn't want me. He didn't want to pay the fee that I wanted in order to be brought in and he didn't want me. He had a complaining witness and four other women that were testifying in that case, but the lawyer who was representing him said, 'You need her, you've got to have her.' And I can remember going to — he was a minister. I can remember going to his house, and he had a glass of wine and gave me a look, and I knew. I knew that's what happened with those women at his house. The prosecutor said, 'Never be alone with him, never be alone with him,' right? And he ultimately hired me and we got an acquittal in that case. He wanted to hug me after that, and I wouldn't have any part of hugging him. But he didn't see that he needed a woman in that case, but the male lawyer did. And so whenever there's a child or a repeat offender or a molestation, you've got to have a woman because a jury doesn't fear that man as much if I, as a woman, would sit next to him, touch him, defend him, whatever."

"Let me ask what I think might be in some of our audience members' minds. Does that feel weird to you, like, sort of taking advantage or game playing? I'm not exactly sure how to ask the question, but do you know what I mean?" I ask.

"Yeah. Maybe it is, but it never felt that way to me because it was important to get for the client what would give them the best chance of getting a just trial, a fair trial. And if it meant that — I mean, it's not unlike having a client put glasses on, right, or dress well or have a haircut. Prosecutors do that all the time. One prosecutor taught me to bring the Girl Scout cookie box and set it on the table. She would do that during trial. And I said, 'Why do you have that Girl Scout cookie box?' And she said, 'Because I want that jury to see it. Either they think I'm a scout mom or I bought a lot of cookies. Either way,

The Feminine Sixth: Women for the Defense

I get something out of it.' So I had a Girl Scout cookie box in a rape case. I don't think there's anything wrong with that."

"Can you talk about this from a racial as well as gender perspective?"

"Well, I have gotten it from everywhere," Cynthia responds. "Colleagues, clients, judges, you name it." She pauses to think. "Well, clients have said, 'I think the white lawyer might know the judge,' and somehow they think that he'll get a favor, right? And they think that men — I don't know — whatever it is that we value in our society about men more than women, right, they thought men would do better. And I think part of it has to do with the bonding with men and being able to tell a man the truth about what happened, right? So, many of the criminal defense lawyers in Atlanta would meet their clients in a strip club, somewhere I would not be comfortable meeting them."

"That's interesting. It sounds like you actually had conversations with clients about gender and race and that sort of thing, direct conversations."

"Um-hum. Absolutely," she replies.

"Do you know that most criminal defense lawyers don't ever do that?" I ask.

"No, I did not," Cynthia laughs ruefully.

"So how did you figure out to do that?" asks Amanda.

"I have conversations with most people about that, so clients wouldn't be any different for me. You spend enough time with the person and eventually you get around to those subjects. So I guess I've spent enough time with clients to get there." Cynthia replies.

"The way you say this is it just seems natural to you to do, and I'm just telling you it's not natural. Almost nobody ever, ever says a word about any of those subjects, especially not with clients," Lisa says.

"Wow." Cynthia shakes her head.

"I can certainly remember times where I had conversations with a client where I would say, 'I'm worried because,' and I would talk about the racial issue or the gang issue or the tattoo issue or whatever the issue was that was worrying me. And there would be this moment — most of the time, not every client responded like this, but most of the time, there would be this moment of just relief that it was on the table," I say. I see some agreement from the panel, but not uniformly.

"Well, I guess for me, if you're talking to a client about trial strategy, you have to talk about the fact that I'm a woman; I'm a lawyer and I'm a woman, right, which makes a difference. I'm a lawyer and I'm a black woman, and your jury is likely to look somewhat different, and here you are with me. I mean, you have to talk about that," says Cynthia, nonplussed.

"Well, actually, no, you don't. You would be shocked how unusual that is," I say.

"The argument on the other side is that we burn out, and if we care too much, we can't see clearly and you need to have some distance. I'm sure you've heard this from male colleagues

The Feminine Sixth: Women for the Defense

and probably some women colleagues, too, which leads me to another question, which is: When you indicate that you sometimes operate through your feelings as opposed to your thoughts, or in addition to your thoughts, do you think that's in any way related to your gender or to your race, or do you feel like this is just something that can happen to anyone?"

"I think it can happen to anyone if they're open to it. I think women are socialized to be more open to it, and I think as an African American, I'm socialized to be more open to it, right? To allow it to happen, to not be ashamed of it happening. So since the social mores allow me to feel, I feel more often, I think, as a woman and as an African American woman. I think men can do it, but the value of it for them is diminished and it's subjugated to thinking and appearing to be in control, and those sorts of things. And we have those pressures. But if we lose it, somehow there's permission for — I have permission to cry with my client in the courtroom. I don't think many men do. And I think that's the difference," Cynthia answers.

"Well, what about the other side of it when you've got to basically kick somebody's butt?" asks Huma.

"So it takes a different shape for me, because many clients, male clients particularly because they're mostly male clients, have to fit you into some category, I think. You're certainly not a lover, you can be a sister sometimes, and you can be a mom or an aunt sometimes. So depending on how I perceive they fit me into a category or into what category, that's the approach I use for being stern. So if I see that they — by the questions they ask and how they interact with me, if they see me as this older mother/aunt-type figure, then I can say to them, 'Now, you know you need to do this and you know that's right,' you know, as a mother would. But if they see me in this peer, sort of sister/cousin place, then it's, 'Listen, you know, I think we really need to think about this and we really need....' — You know? There's a different approach to it, but it's the same sternness, it's the same guiding them to the decision that they need to make in their own best interest. But there's a different approach depending on how they see you as that woman lawyer."

I step in. "It's interesting, because Huma's question was if you had to kick someone's butt, and you immediately assumed client. But what I think she meant was what about if there's a police officer on the stand and you need to cross-examine him into submission? I have felt at times that while in movies and such, they enjoy having women heroes doing karate kicking and whatever else, that there's some level where it's sort of not ladylike to take on a cop or a criminalist or whatever." I look at Huma. "Was that right?" I ask her. She nods.

"So I'm Southern, and so on top of that layer of ladylike, there's the Southernicity."

"Southernicity? All right. A new word," I respond.

"Not to me," quips Cynthia Stewart.

"There is the idea that there's politeness in being Southern, but frankly, that really works," Cynthia Roseberry continues. "The National Criminal Defense College taught me that there's not one way to do it, right, to skin a cat. And so I found that by being kind and stern in cross-examinations, when I can, when I need to, I get far more — as my mother would say, you get more flies with honey than you do with vinegar, right? There are times when I've had to be tough, and I think that plays out as a woman in the courtroom with the jury looking at that cop, saying, 'Why are you beating up on that woman?' sometimes. And that's a sexism, frankly, that works for the benefit of our clients sometimes. I've had times where witnesses have come back at me and I've gone back at them, but I think that was earlier in my career before I knew — before I felt comfortable knowing that there's more than one way to do it."

"Have you had any experiences, or could you describe maybe two different times where you have felt that your gender and/or your race have worked against you, one where it was salient, where it was clear, and one where you could feel it, but you can't prove it? Do you know what I mean?" I ask.

"Sure. Other than being told by an African American male U.S. Marshal that the defendant's girlfriend could not sit at counsel table — when I entered the room, and in the Batman case, the pimping case, when the government used a lot of the clothing as exhibits, a judge right before closing argument invited me to use any of those as demonstrative evidence if I wanted to, you know, thigh-high boots and sexy clothes."

"Seriously?" I query.

"Yes. You said against me, not for me, right?"

"Well, either way."

"So I can remember a case where I had an African American client who was accused of exposing himself in a library, and they actually charged him with aggravated assault because when he got in his car to pull out, a woman had chased him to get his tag and they felt he tried to back the car into her, right? So we're at trial, and the client had not told me about this belt that he was supposed to have had and how they probably confused his penis with the belt. You know, it was this long belt, and he pulled it out, the belt, in trial for the first time on cross-examination with a Caucasian district attorney." Cynthia laughs. "And the client says, 'Maybe they thought it was my belt,' and he pulls it out. And he says, 'Have you ever told your lawyer about this belt?' 'No.' So the DA picks up the belt, and it's a really long belt, and holds it up in front of the jury and says to the client, 'I've never seen a penis that was long enough to be confused with this belt, have you?' or something like that, to the client. And the client didn't answer. But there were a couple of African American women in the jury, so I looked over at them and gave them this little smirk, and they smirked back and kind of moved their heads the way we do, and I just let the prosecutor continue." She laughs again.

"They couldn't convict that client. . . so I felt that was a way in which I was an African American woman who connected with those jurors in that way, you know, playing the race card, as they say, that was to the benefit of my client."

I nod to Huma. "Huma, would you please talk about your experiences? I think we would like to hear your perspective as a woman, a woman of color, and also as a Muslim woman defense lawyer."

"Is that all?" asks Huma, laughing quietly. I smile back. Okay that is a really BIG question.

"Let me start by describing how I got here. I grew up in a relatively low-income Boston suburb. It was interesting just because being in public school, there were no kids that looked like me. Mattapan used to be a very white elder community. The demographics are very white, older, usually retirees. But then it kind of started shifting and it became younger and more African American predominantly, a lot of African immigrants, so, like, Haitians and Dominicans, especially on our street, but it was a low-income area."

The Feminine Sixth: Women for the Defense

"So my dad had applied to get me into the Sharon METCO, M-E-T-C-O, Program, which bused kids from the lower-income suburbs to the higher-income suburbs. It was kind of a lottery system. Suddenly I got to go to school in Hingham and in Newton, which were relatively wealthy, very, very white districts, to the point that I was the only nonwhite person in my class, which was not a good thing. I don't recommend any child be the only anything in their classes in those years. I went to school with very wealthy, very white kids who knew for sure that I was not either of those things. Then we moved to the Chicago area and I went to Glenbard South and I still covered my hair. So I was probably one of maybe two, two or three kids max, in the public high school that did that, and it was fine. Then a couple of weeks later, September 11th happened."

"My mom came and got me that day, the morning of September 11th of 2001, and she brought me home because no one really knew what was going on. So by 10:30, 11:00 o'clock, I was at home watching the news. My best friend who was still at my old private school, her mom dropped her off at my house, and we just spent the whole day watching the news. My parents kept me home from school the next day, and on that day, my dad was, like, 'You know, I don't think you should wear the hijab anymore.' In our culture, in our family dynamics, certainly when my dad says, 'I think,' or 'I suggest,' or 'It would be a good idea if,' that's interpreted as 'Do this.' So that was really disturbing to me, but I did it. I went back to school, I think, on September 13th without my hijab. I mean, it was horrible for me just because it was — it was very 'other-izing,' and I felt very exposed in many different ways, because I knew by that time who had done — who had committed the attacks of September 11th."

There is a silence as we all digest this; how Huma had experienced that day.

"There are some obvious ways in which our culture differs. For example, culturally we don't — my parents would be very troubled if I wore a knee-length dress with pantyhose or without pantyhose, that would be a thing that they would not be comfortable with that they would let me know was not acceptable. As silly as it sounds to get into the particulars of it, amazingly enough, tights, they're on the fence about. It's just that I know what's expected of me, given my culture, my background, my religion, my parents' interpretation of all those things, because there are plenty of Muslim parents who have no problem with those things and plenty of Muslim parents who have a huge problem with leggings or tights who are way more conservative than my parents. But based on what I knew about my parents' interpretations of those things, I knew that they would be horrified if I wore a strapless or a knee-length dress without anything underneath covering my legs."

She stops for a moment.

"The rest of your big question, about being a woman, well, I think about that sometimes when it gets a bit tough because I always have those doubts. Women talk a lot about imposter syndrome, that we always question ourselves as to whether we really know what we're doing, whether we have the mettle for it. I think about that a lot when things get tough, but I always come to the conclusion that, yes, I'm doing this for a reason, I'm here for a reason, I can handle what gets thrown at me. And I tend to think of those now as just periods of doubt that I can overcome."

The Feminine Sixth: Women for the Defense

"Do you find that being a Muslim directly impacts your work?" asks Juanita, leaning forward, fascinated.

"Well sometimes it does, when my belief is clearly not the same as the client or his family. Don't get me wrong, it is wonderful to have that personal belief, but it doesn't translate very well in Cook County–Chicago courts. Cook County doesn't care if Jesus is on your side. There was this woman (the mother of a client) who would hug me whenever I walked into court to be on her case, and she was always very nice in person and she'd hug me when she'd leave. Then one day she called the office and she told our paralegal something that really troubled her, so she got our secretary to witness the call. Basically, this woman said that she wanted my boss to appear in court with her because I was not Christian and I didn't walk with Jesus, and she felt that Raymond, my boss, should be with her because Raymond is a good Catholic boy. So they were kind of nervous to tell me because they thought, 'How are we going to bring that up with her, that this crazy person is saying you're not good enough to be her son's attorney because you're not Christian?' So I listened, and I said, 'Well, that doesn't surprise me, not even remotely.' It was what it was. Raymond was very upset about it and we dealt with it. He would occasionally come to court with me from then on. We took it to trial, and it was a not guilty. What I learned from that is that there are just some people who have prejudices who are very nice to your face, but have prejudices, and you deal with it. I didn't stop being her son's attorney just because she didn't think I was Christian enough. That's not how it works."

"It would be great if you could share anything interesting or surprising concerning these issues that you've discovered over the course of your career," I ask.

"I've been very lucky in my life as a person of color, because obviously a person of color has experiences with law enforcement that are different than a white person from birth. It's just the nature of the whole situation." Huma takes a deep breath. "So when Sesame Street tells us that if you're ever in trouble, go find a police officer, that might not be something that a black parent tells their child, you know. A white parent will tell their kid, 'If you ever get lost, go find a policeman and he'll help you find me.' A black parent might not say that because they don't view police officers with the same sense of security. I also find that people underestimate me all the time because of my gender and because of my youth and my appearance, I guess, in general, because I am rather diminutive."

There are appreciative chuckles in the audience — they have seen her nearly on the tips of her toes to reach the microphone.

"Also I look very young. I get mistaken for someone who is 18, 19, 20, which still surprises me. But when I walk into a courtroom, especially my first two years, and it still happens now, but more so back then, courtroom personnel would literally ask me if I was lost. I would be sitting at defense counsel table in a suit with a file that is clearly a court file, and they would say, 'Excuse me. Are you lost?' And the judges never expected much out of me in the way of a fight, in the way of advocating for my client or trying to maneuver something, they never expected much out of me just from the get-go. So when I did put up a fight, when I did say, 'But, Judge, what about. . .' that raised some brows."

"I get underestimated a lot, by opposing counsel especially. My opposing counsel are usually tall, white, and male. So one of the funniest experiences was once I had a hearing against a young, tall, six-foot-two, broad-shouldered man's man of

The Feminine Sixth: Women for the Defense

a prosecutor, and I made the choice to put my hair up in a ponytail, which I know makes me look young, and wear flats, and do the hearing that way. So I came up probably to his — a little above his elbow. It worked. Well, it worked for a lot of different reasons, because I had good case law on my side, because I had prepared, and I had a good motion and all that. But the judge was also a woman who was five-one, and she always laughed at the height difference between me and him, too. So it was all those little things. I'm underestimated a lot, more so when I just started, but certainly now. And I like that, I prefer that, because that gives me room to rise, room to show what I can do. So I like that aspect of it. I make the joke obviously that the legal profession is still something of a boy's club and most criminal defense attorneys are men, and it's very much that mentality."

Huma stops for a moment, I look at her to see if she is finished, but she holds up a finger, "One more thing. Oddly enough, I am a cautionary tale in my community, because, like I said, I am 29, I am still unmarried, and in our community, that's a bit unusual. And the idea is if a woman goes through further schooling, if she pursues a profession, the insinuation is this is something that will make her more marriageable, because a woman who is a doctor, who has that earning potential, is a more attractive spouse than a woman who has an associate's degree. It's horrible to say it that way because it sounds so transactional, but that's what it is, that's the reality of it. I've seen that play out over and over in my own peer group as far as my Muslim friends. Relatively few women in our community make it to 29 without being married. In fact, it's viewed as 'What's wrong with her?' and it's kind of a mark of shame or whatever."

"Well we are going to talk a bit more about those pressures after lunch, but let me ask you now, does that worry you?"

"Not much," she says with emphasis.

"Crystal," I say, "can you come talk to us about this now?"

"Sure," she says, approaching the podium. "Although I don't know that I have that much to say directly about these subjects that hasn't been said. A challenge for me was how does a professional woman behave? How does she dress and carry herself?"

Crystal nods at the rest of the panel.

"I think we spend a lot more time thinking about what to wear, and what we look like than men, don't you?" There are nods of agreement. "I think I learned a little bit about how to present yourself as a woman professional from my first supervisor in the Santa Clara public defender's office I started in. She was very well-respected by the judges, and yet she had that kind of free spirit that makes a public defender a public defender, and I loved that office. It was a great office. And the other person who was in that office who became a real valuable resource to me was Bryan Shechmeister. One of the things I learned from him, I think, was just that gravitas can matter, just how serious you are about your work can matter, and it can translate in your presented work, you know, whether it's what a judge thinks of you or what a jury thinks of you, because that's what he had. He had gravitas."

"Do you feel like there's some subjects that are — I don't want to say forbidden, but that are difficult to bring up in court or that you find personally difficult to bring up in the context of working on a case?" I ask.

"Like what?"

The Feminine Sixth: Women for the Defense

"Well, as we have discussed already today some lawyers say that they never, ever bring up the issue of race for example."

"Well, it's really part of jury work, isn't it? I mean, wow. Hmm. Maybe you talk to a judge differently than you talk to jurors, but I think if there's an issue that you're afraid of — and I think I learned this from you — if there's an issue you're afraid of, you'd better be talking about it. Even if you say, 'I'm really afraid of this issue, but can you talk to me about it,' to a juror, you've got to be talking about it. And here's what I've learned from that, and I know that you're the person who taught me that, and I just don't remember what case it was. It may not have been a case that we were doing together, but more a case where I was watching you work. So maybe it was even a death case or something. But, anyway, watching jury selection and watching you really — you know, when we talk about that kind of thing to jurors, who are just these people sitting there, we don't know anything about them. We're all on the line. I mean, it is like the first time you stand up to teach a class. Everything about you is out there, everything. You are naked out there talking to these people on behalf of some guy who is sitting behind you who can't talk about that and maybe wouldn't talk about that, but you have to. Sometimes it's sex. Sometimes if you're doing a terrible sexual assault case, you've got to talk about sex, you've got to talk about consent."

"I do remember a case in Santa Clara where there was no way this was a consent case, but it's all I had." Crystal nods at the audience. "One of the things about criminal defense is, sometimes, you have to put on a defense, because that is what there is, not because you like it." I see the panelists nodding. She continues. "The woman had — it was one of — it was my first serious felony tour in Santa Clara, and this sexual assault case was part of the caseload that I took over. A father and in-his-20s son are standing outside of their car early one morning; they're getting ready to go to work together, I think, and they're just standing outside of the car talking before they get in the car to go to work. They look up and they see a woman — they see the window to a home flung open from the second story, and a naked woman comes flying out, lands on the ground, gets up, and starts running towards them, yelling, 'Help me, help me. I've been raped.'"

"Oh, for God's sake," I say.

"So the woman really was filled with drugs, but — so there I was. I mean, I learned early on that if you had one single fact that became the theory of your case. And so, of course, I had to talk to a jury about whether — about what 'consent' means, what 'consent' means in a sexual context and, you know, what about consent now and feeling bad about it later or all the things that can happen. And I remember thinking, 'I can't talk to people about this,' you know, and then I remembered watching you. And I don't know what it was, but it might have been a race issue. You may have been representing a client who was African American and a white victim, and I remember knowing as I sat watching you that you were having the same feeling that I had been having, I'm all out here, I'm hanging out here talking to these people. I don't remember how I felt in my own case, but I remember watching you and thinking, 'She may not be getting this, but they kind of dig that she's asking this because it's real.' And I can't tell you what case it was, so I don't know if you felt it. But you were getting real answers. You were getting real answers. And people were saying, 'Well, I understand why you would think that about me.' And they were talking about their own background that they had told the judge in the answers to the questions, 'I understand why you might think that about me.' And I thought, you know, the thing about

The Feminine Sixth: Women for the Defense

being naked in front of people is they'll try to help you. The ones you want on the jury will try to help you."

"Yeah. They will. They will," I say.

"So that gives you a little — I don't know if it's courage or — I don't know what it is. But it gives you the ability to ask people tough questions because you are — you're not asking them where they get their news, right? You're asking them something that really matters, however they answer it." Crystal looks around, and nods at the audience. She can feel that they *heard* her.

"Hey, Amanda," I say, "you're up."

"Well, let me start here. When I went to college, I had a picture that I had in a frame in my freshman dorm of my high school at the beach, and in the picture it was white, black, Latino, Asian, Filipino at the beach, and to me that was 100 percent normal, but then people from other areas would comment on it, and that's when I realized it wasn't normal to have such exposure to a wide array of people, a diverse population living in a place like Victorville. I remember I had a friend in my freshman dorm who said something like, 'I don't know if there were that many brown people in my whole high school.' There were some more offensive ones that were like, 'Oh, did you go to the' — I don't remember what they said. I'm trying to remember. I don't remember what they — it was something kind of offensive like, 'Did you go to the immigrant club and take this picture?' or something like that."

"Oh, for goodness sake," I say. I see heads shaking in the audience.

"Yeah. I don't know if those were the exact words, but it was one of those things that make you — it made me, at least, especially as a white woman, feel very uncomfortable and very out of place. I felt really lucky because I — my high school was in the bottom third of California high schools. So at the time, the UC, the University of California system, and UC San Diego specifically, had a program where if you went to one of the bottom third of high schools and you got in to UC San Diego, you could participate in kind of like a kick-starter program the month before school started, and it was a retention program for first-time college-goers, first generation college goers, to try to kind of prepare you for the academic rigor of a school like UCSD, kind of acknowledging that perhaps your high school didn't prepare you as well as your colleagues would be prepared coming in. I think that was for me huge, not just academically, but also politically and personally because I made my best friends in that program. It was called Summer Bridge, that program before school started. I think that was kind of the beginning of me becoming more radicalized and more critical in my thought, especially political thought."

"Why was that?"

"Because one of the classes — I was one of two white students who participated in the program out of, I think there were, I don't know, maybe 80 of us. And part of the program was we took a class on privilege, and I think it was giving permission to students of color to study and legitimize these concepts. For me, it was nothing I had been exposed to in high school; we never got that far. So getting to study that and learn about that right away, and also being in the environment that I was in with other students of color and learning from them and really sharing a lot with them, it was a very intensive program. We had a lot of group time and processing. I feel like I just grew so much in that month, and I got to hear from other people what their experiences were like. Then turning from that to being spilled out into the 40,000-person campus where most people there had parents, grandparents, who went to college, had friends, 20 or 30 friends, from their graduating class that came to that school, it was a very eye-opening contrast, those two — I guess two different kinds of exposure to different kinds of people."

"The diversity of the paths we've all taken is truly remarkable," I observe. "I want to return to the issue of gender because one of the things that we can all see is that you're kind of a stunning strawberry blond." Amanda laughs, a little self-conscious.

"I'm not trying to be funny here," I continue. "It's been very interesting how women perceive that their looks helped or hurt them and their gender helped or hurt them, and I'm wondering if you could talk a little bit about that and maybe give an example or two of whatever it is, conclusions that you've come to."

"Okay," she begins. "Yeah, I think to say that the way someone looks doesn't impact how they're treated or perceived or how they're received would be just to — I don't even know. It would just be utter denial of how humans operate. So I think there's a big part of me that can't wait until I get some gray hairs because I think that might bring some credibility. I feel as a young woman that I am not taken seriously. Sometimes when I'm looking for critical feedback, I can't even get that."

"Can you tell me more about that?"

"I think sometimes I ask questions and I ask them very seriously and literally, and people that I work with are taking it as I'm looking for — I don't know — praise or fluff or something like that, and I'm really trying to improve as a professional. I can think of one time that I tried a case, and I was kind of a third chair with a man and a woman who don't normally work together. When I asked the man, who was the first chair, an older white man, what he thought about something I did, he said, 'You're doing fine, sweetheart.' Then when I asked the woman, she said, 'You need to go back and fix this and this, and here's why,' and she really helped me. I guess it could be just two humans acting differently, but I get so much more growth and true feedback from female mentors. That's not to say that I haven't had really great male mentors, but on the whole, I think I grow more when I work with other women, experienced women."

"I wanted to talk with you, Amanda, about the role that your gender plays with clients, and particularly some of the racial dynamics of that, which you've spoken about some before. But a fact of life is that a lot of clients in Chicago, certainly mine and certainly yours, are people of color and mostly men. I'm wondering if you could talk a little bit about navigating that."

"I think something that I've tried to be really purposeful about is having a certain level of curiosity and naiveté when I approach a client about their experiences and not just their experiences, but maybe their case or their upbringing or something like that, because I think it's helpful not to assume and not to put people in categories. They very well might be putting me in a category about where I come from or what I've seen, but I'm not going to do that to them. Seeing each client as an individual, everyone has a story of struggle; you do, I do, we all do. I think especially in federal representation, my biggest goal is to figure out what one person, my client's, story of struggle is, and it's not going to be the same across the board just because they're men or just because they are black or Latino."

The Feminine Sixth: Women for the Defense

Amanda pauses, and takes a deep breath. "Every single person is going to have a different story of struggle. I think it's important to expose — I guess self-disclose and recognize privilege and try to — I think once you recognize privilege, you can empower your clients. So recognizing my white privilege is important, something that I'm working on. I think it's difficult. I think there's a level of distrust coming in as a white female public defender. There's a level of probably appropriate distrust because I'm just another person who looks a lot like everyone else, who looks a lot like the guards, who looks a lot like the judge, who looks a lot like the prosecutor. So I think that there's a lot of work to be done to earn trust, and I think part of that is just shutting the hell up and listening. I do think that actions speak louder than words. You can tell someone, look, I know we come from different places, I know this. But if you can't stand up in court and tell someone's story with dignity and get other people to understand why it's important, then your client's not really going to feel like all that lip service means anything. I don't know if I'm making any sense."

I look at Juanita. It's her turn and she takes the hint. "Oh you are making sense alright," she says.

"Let me start with the National Criminal Defense College. For those of you who don't know, it's a trial practice program for criminal defense lawyers, the faculty are the best in the country, and you work in small groups with paradigm cases and actors playing witnesses, and learn how to be a better lawyer. You are divided up into small groups based on your experience — from A to L, A being most experienced. Which, two weeks in Macon, Georgia in the summer, well that is literally the hot house effect. When I went I hadn't had that much trial experience, so I wasn't in A group or B group or anything, and apparently people talked about, okay, this woman is going to be a superstar."

"Isn't that lovely?" I smile.

"Deserved or not it was wonderful. And they were clearly looking to add women and minorities to the faculty because back then it was Jim Shellow, Gerry Spence, Garvin Isaacs, John Ackerman, Jim Doherty, Terry McCarthy. Do you hear me naming any African American, anyone of color?"

"No."

"Anyone of color or any women?"

"No. There weren't any," I respond.

"So clearly I stood out for them for lots of reasons," Juanita continues. "A, I was really good; and, B, I was a two for one, a woman and Hispanic. So I was invited back as faculty the very next year. Now, all my colleagues at the highly regarded San Diego federal defenders, all the guys, had been there as participants. None of them had been invited back as faculty, not one. And they were all way older than me. They were pissed. Now, there was the first time I saw it. I came back. I got invited by John Ackerman, who was the dean at the time. And I didn't get invited right then. Obviously, they must have talked about it, and a while later I get a call from John inviting me to come back the next year as faculty. I'm so excited, and I go tell these guys that I think are my friends. And one of them says to me, 'So who did you blow?' And what really hurt the most is I think a part of them actually believed it. They actually believed there's no way I would have been invited back as faculty unless I had either slept with somebody or blew somebody who then pulled some strings to get his girlfriend back as faculty."

"Wow," Cyndy Short says. "Not that I am surprised." She pauses. "Much."

"It never occurred to them that how about just *maybe* it's because I'm that fricking good? So part of them, I think, actually really believed it, and part of it was they were just jealous, which I didn't realize at the time but have since come to see, that as I advanced and advanced and they didn't in their careers, I'm sure it — rather than be super happy for me, there was a part of it that was like, seriously? This fricking girl?"

"It's complicated. And there's this, like, oh, it's 'affirmative action.'" I make my words syrupy. "Not necessarily those words, but that sort of thing, that that's what — it's got to be about."

"Which means you don't deserve it," Juanita responds.

"Right. It can't be just because you're good enough. Yeah. I had a streak in Task Force. Every now and then you have a streak, right? And I got something like seven acquittals in a row or something like that, six or seven. I just had a streak. I haven't had one since, not like that, but I just did. And the rumor was I slept my way to all these acquittals."

I am laughing by now. So is Juanita.

"That's a lot of jurors," she says.

"I know. That's 12 jurors and two alternates..." We are really laughing now, and so is the audience.

"Exhausting," says Juanita, very languidly.

"Not to mention a few judges. And no one saw. You know, men, women, dogs, cats, who knew? Anyway, it's hard to explain how painful it is to feel run down that way, and it makes you wonder, was I seeing this person clearly in the first place. I don't know if I'm saying that very well." I am trying not to show just how much it *hurt*, even though I can laugh now.

"No. I understand exactly what you're saying, because it's your colleagues, for God's sake. It's okay if — well, it's not okay, but you expect like your enemies, your opposition or something to want to take shots at you. But when your own colleagues crap on you that way, it is very painful," says Juanita.

"So you went into private practice after about three years, and talk a little bit about what that was like, especially as the only woman," I ask.

"Again, it's just so funny because I had tried the rape/murder case with the federal protective officer, I had done big cases. And now I go into private practice and I went in with some former federal defenders in the same building, and these guys were treating me like I was a law clerk. They were all referring cases to each other, and they would ask me did I want to make $10 an hour doing legal research for them." She shakes her head.

"A theme we have already talked about is how things look and how they appear. And if you don't mind me saying so, one of the assets that you have is that you're gorgeous."

"Oh, thank you," answers Juanita.

The Feminine Sixth: Women for the Defense

"Well, it's true. And you always have been. And that is a plus in some ways, but I bet it's also a negative in some ways in terms of being a professional. I think, personally, that not being traditionally pretty — I am not being self-deprecatory here — but I am a big six foot tall woman who is more handsome than pretty — has helped me skirt some of those issues. Could you talk about that just a bit? You don't need to be modest here. This is pure, objective fact."

"Well, thank you, Andrea. I don't think of myself that way, but you know how women are, they never think of themselves as how other people might see them. It was a detriment in that there would be times — there would be big disappointments. There would be times when I would meet a lawyer that I thought valued and respected me. It turned out all they wanted to do was get in my pants. That was very depressing to find that. And each time it happened, it was like, seriously? I thought you wanted to sit next to me at dinner because you heard about my latest win. And the funny thing is that the one person, the one male who was already a big deal lawyer who believed in me unequivocally and believed that I could become the greatest criminal defense lawyer ever, was Michael Pancer — always believed in me one hundred percent, and it wasn't to get into my pants, although I'm sure he would have loved to, and now does."

We both laugh. "Michael is her husband," I tell the audience.

"He really believed in me. But there were so many others that I thought did, but it turned out that was all it was. Then as far as the clients, I don't think looks got in the way. Youth got in the way sometimes. But one thing I learned, do not put up with people denigrating you and taking you less seriously because you're a woman in a man's profession. I hope it's changing in the criminal defense world. I see more and more women. Back in my day, there were very few. There's still very few in the patent world, for example, the patent litigation world. I put up with way too much shit. I let guys talk trash to me that I never should have done, but I thought I needed to get along, let them be rude and offensive and demeaning and denigrating because instead of calling them on it and just calling it bullshit and saying, 'Stop it, that's totally inappropriate; you're behaving like a pig,' and 'Do it again and you're going to hurt somewhere.'"

I see nods from the panel, and I know it is time to take a lunch break. So I tell the audience that is what we are going to do. "When we come back, we are going to talk about confronting moral repugnance in our work, and then work/life balance, and, finally, why we are still standing." Everyone starts heading for the door. I have lunch waiting for the panelists in the 'green room' (which is actually not green).

CHAPTER FOUR:
CONFRONTING MORAL REPUGNANCE

"How can you represent those people?!" I say in a loud voice as we gather again after lunch.

"This is a question we get in one form or another all the time. It's not just limited to women criminal defense lawyers, it's to everyone, but we often get our own particular brand of the question. So the panel is going to discuss their answers to this question, and whether or not they feel that their answers are different — or the question is different — because of being women."

Cynthia Roseberry starts the conversation. "So it varies, of course, but it's interesting to me that it seems that people generally are more interested in my opinion about things once they know that I'm a lawyer and in particular that I'm a criminal defense lawyer. You inevitably get the question: 'How do you represent those people?' 'Have you ever represented anybody you know who was guilty?' Those kinds of questions. They seem to be pretty interested. Many times I get asked if I'm afraid of my clients, and I'm not sure if men are asked that question."

"I am not sure," I say.

"Probably not very often," says Cynthia Stewart.

Cynthia Roseberry continues, "You know, I can say there's maybe one client that I've ever been afraid of, and that was just because of mental illness more than any sort of malice or anything like that. But that question strikes me as interesting. And then there's the 'How do you represent those people?' question that always comes up."

"Obviously we all get that question quite a bit, but is there something sort of stock that you say? Does it depend on who is asking or how they're requesting?" I respond.

"So I think I have a stock answer." She pauses. "Maybe I have several, depending on who is asking. Maybe somebody who I know is not associated with the military, I might say, we do the same thing as soldiers, we defend the Constitution of the United States, right? And some people can kind of get that. If it's somebody who appears to be from the same socioeconomic background as the one in which I was reared, I might talk about the idea that people who are poor need a voice, right? And then maybe in larger circles I do talk about ideals, you know, justice and love, as I've spoken about before. But I can say that generally I would say to everyone that I believe that all of us are capable of doing all of the things that all of us do, given the right set of circumstances. And so under our law, that's not a crime until you've been convicted of it, or you're not guilty of a crime until you've been convicted of it, and so everyone deserves that presumption of innocence, because when we start to pick and choose again, guess who doesn't get it? The poor, the despised among us, and that's a direct reflection of who we are. If we don't care for people who can't help us in any way, then what kind of a society are we?"

The Feminine Sixth: Women for the Defense

Christine Start responds, "I have very different politics than my community, and my family. So at first, I got those sort of questions — which weren't really question, you know?" The panelists all nod, so do some audience members. They know. "I remember having a lot of political arguments with my mom. My dad is not a confrontational person, so my mom is a — and, also, another traditional thing about Filipinos is the woman is usually the dominant one in the family."

"Oh, that's interesting. I didn't know that," I say.

"Yeah. We had a Filipina president in the Philippines, so women do play a huge role. They're the center of the family. In my family, it's the same. My grandma, my mom's mom, everybody goes to her for everything. So it was a struggle. I think, one, they just love me, so that helped convince them. But I think media and television, my parents are those people that love to watch TV every night. There are shows that expose what a criminal defense attorney does. During law school, I had a mock trial. I did an intensive advocacy program, and we got to do our first mock jury trial. So I invited my parents to come, and they actually got to sit on the jury. They totally were cool with it. They were just so into it, and they thought my job was pretty hard, you know. Then my mom, I remember — what was it? I think it was my first or second year as a public defender, and she got called to sit on a rape case. She was on the panel. She didn't end up getting selected, but I think she was there about a week while they were doing jury selection. And she told me about it afterwards. She said, 'Gosh, the defense attorney has the hardest job in the room because I get it now.' She just said, 'Everybody needs a lawyer.'"

"Could you tell us about some moral distaste or repugnance or whatever you want to call it toward criminal defense work that you yourself have experienced?" I ask Christine.

"So there was a point a couple of years ago where I had made this decision that I did not want to be a public defender for the rest of my life. I thought that I did when I applied to law school and did everything I did to be a public defender while in law school. But that is not exactly what you mean right? You mean like a case that challenged my beliefs?" I nod.

"Well, there is one that is a good example. I call it my 'media case,' because it's an animal cruelty case, and I thought essentially all it was — you know, it's on video, but her, I guess you could say, friend/roommate, they were having drama, so he decided to blast on Facebook a video, because he had security out of his trailer home, of her in arguments throughout the day with neighbors. Then you see this video of her holding their pug, Benny the pug. His name is Benny; he's named after her boyfriend. You see her and she's holding the dog with one hand. You can't tell if she's holding it with a harness or holding it by its neck or by its paw, kind of hard to tell. But you could tell she's really pissed, and you see her literally chuck the dog towards the boyfriend, and it rolls."

"Oh, boy."

"The dog gets right back up and is wagging his tail and is fine, completely fine, no injuries. Actually, they took it to the clinic, they went to the vet, cleared it, no harm done. He rolled the perfect way he could have rolled, no injuries. But the video looked really bad. It looked so bad on camera, so bad to the point where it was a bad day, the neighbor/friend, ex-friend now, blasts it on Facebook and it goes viral. People in Cape Town, Africa, in Europe, people are petitioning to file criminal charges against her and throw her across the room. She's terrible, she's an animal abuser. She's had this pug for a couple years or something, has another dog, loves her dog. It was a heat of the moment type of thing where her and her boyfriend

The Feminine Sixth: Women for the Defense

were in a very big fight. Actually, prior to that, she was in another fight with another person. So it was just this big thing."

"So what's on video and what's in the police report is this chuck of the dog. What ends up coming out in evidence at prelim — so the DA files felony charges on the woman — felony animal abuse for this unharmed dog, which probably would be a misdemeanor but for the fact that the media blew it up and they put all this pressure on the DA, and the DA made this public statement, and this DA will do whatever looks good in the media eye. So, yeah, with the case, it shouldn't have been filed as a felony, but it was filed as a felony. My client has an anger issue, and she is a victim of domestic violence. They're in a very twisted relationship, this boyfriend of hers. So according to the police reports, according to the witnesses, that's what happened, she chucked the dog. So we have the prelim. So, mind you, a week or two weeks before this, she ends up getting arrested for a domestic violence incident where her boyfriend called the police on her, the same one she was in a fight with on the video, for trying to stab him with a Samurai sword."

"A Samurai sword?" says Cynthia Stewart. "That's unusual." There are murmurs and chuckles.

Christine nods ruefully. "Yup. A Samurai sword. So now she's in custody. On the animal abuse case he bailed her out, but this time around, now that he files a strike offense against her for trying to stab him with a Samurai sword, the bail is too high. She can't get out, so she's in now. The DA says, 'Oh, we'll dismiss this strike offense against a human being and all that as long as she pleads to the animal count.' It's all because a sword on an ex with a record, no problem, but an unharmed dog, well that's another."

"Have any of you had experiences, specific ones, where there was a clear element of moral repugnance for you — sort of like Crystal's rape case she discussed earlier that you would be willing to discuss?" I ask.

Lisa Wayne speaks up. "I had been out of the public defender's office maybe a year and a half, and I was not accepting state court appointments because I felt like I had done my time. But Bert Nieslanik, who is an incredible lawyer and also someone who has been inspiring throughout my career called me to help. She was someone I could not turn down, and I had been so lucky. I got to work with all of these incredible women in the Colorado public defender system that are great, just great lawyers. So I was asked to take this awful gang rape case that had occurred in Boulder. This is a case involving Hmong defendants, the first really big one in Colorado."

"What is Hmong?" I ask.

"So it's H-m-o-n-g. The Hmong were Vietnamese who were used by the CIA and the military to turn against their own people in the Vietnam war. Once the war was over, we had to get them out of there. These are rural people who had been farmers and peasants. Some of them had been in the military, but, on the whole, that's what they really did. So once the war ended, they were obviously considered traitors. So we, the American people, had to get them out of there and we brought them to the United States because they were a displaced people in their own country. They put them in Sacramento, Wisconsin, Minnesota — those are the three largest communities, and we have a very small community in Colorado, so my client actually came from Sacramento — and told them to assimilate. Yeah. That's the typical American way: Come to our country and assimilate and figure it out. So a very interesting culture and I learned about it as a result of the case. So these guys were all living in the same community, and, as many immigrants, hang out with the same family members and would all do the same things together. My client actually had a pretty decent job. He was educated to the extent he had done a couple years of community college and was working at Level 3 which is a software company in Colorado. He and his friends were — and I can say they did it because he was convicted and the appeals have been over many years, but they came to Boulder and they were supposedly in a gang because there was more than a couple of them, and they had a van and they picked up this young female coed off the street about 2:00 o'clock in the morning, and literally picked her off the street; her sandals were left in place, and took her up into the mountains and gang raped her. So it was awful, as you can imagine."

"She was white?" I ask.

"Yes, she was white. She later became a prosecutor."

"Oh, she did?"

"Yes. That's a different story. So Boulder, the liberal community of Boulder, Colorado, wanted blood. And the DA at the time decided that she was going to — Mary Keenan had actually become well known in the country for being an advocate on sex assault cases and had kind of made a niche amongst district attorneys around the country on her advocacy for sexual assault victims. She was one of the few prosecutors during that time who actually put her victims on at the preliminary hearing, not only so they could see how the process went, but she could see how strong they would hold up. So she was very ballsy in many ways. I didn't like a lot of the way she came at things and how she was really rabid about some of these cases, but she actually made some great strides for women on sexual assault cases. So she decided she was going to try the case, and she was running for office at the same time. All the other lawyers that got appointed were Boulder lawyers, and at that point in time, there was a very good old boy community in Boulder, too, where it was lawyers who had tried cases in Boulder. And Boulder still kind of remains that way, there are Boulder lawyers and then there's the rest of us."

"So I did the case and my client was considered one of the leaders. Ultimately I — there was another woman, Nancy Holton, who left the public defender's office, and she had one of the defendants, so she was one of the true believers like me. But I went to trial first. My judge was a fantastic woman who had adopted a Chinese daughter and who is gay, Carol Kalinowski, who was fantastic, she's retired. And I had tried to move the venue a ton of times. You know, had done the polling, done all the things you're supposed to do, and, too bad, you're staying here. After a week of jury selection where it was clear we couldn't get a fair jury in Boulder, Colorado, where the racism was so incredibly prevalent, we spent a week in chambers with I don't know how many jurors. That was just an incredible jury selection, and she, the judge, broke down at the end of it because she realized how prevalent racism against Asians were in this liberal white community where she had adopted a Chinese daughter. It had a huge impact on Carol. Finally we got a change of venue."

"Did you feel that you were treated differently because of your gender or race in this case?"

"Well, I do know it's hard for men to feel what a woman feels about cases like this. And I certainly could feel the weight of that. Maybe they think about their daughters or their wives, but they don't think about that happening to

The Feminine Sixth: Women for the Defense

them as being vulnerable as a victim. I've been threatened by clients, I've been threatened by family members. I've had to have security on cases. I think that there's much more — I don't know. Maybe that's not true, though. When I was in Alabama trying that case in front of Judge Thompson, I had to have security because it was the Ku Klux Klan that was threatening me. But I've had women's groups threaten me on these sex assault cases."

"Can you tell me a story about one of those cases?" I ask.

"I was a public defender, and it's not called NOW, but it's the advocate for sex assault. I can't think of what their name is. It was not, 'We're coming up and we're going to kill you,' but, 'You doing this is putting back the movement, and how could you do this?' Then being in the courtroom and having their presence there, following me out of the court, that's threatening."

"We might think about that more. I tried a murder case when I was pregnant with Dylan, Aaron Bernal, and I was probably seven months pregnant and we walked Aaron on that case, my co-counsel, Pam David, and I. And I walked out of the courthouse and the mother of the victim followed me out. The sheriffs were all by her because they could tell that she was very threatening, and the rest of the family, the victim's family, was there. She came over and she'd put her hand up over my belly and said, 'I curse your child and hope what happened to' — yeah. I remember before Dylan was born, that weighed heavily on me."

"Oh, my goodness."

"So I think you go through some traumatic stuff. I don't know if that happens to men."

I respond, "I don't know either. When I worked as co-counsel on Casey Anthony with Jose Baez, he got attacked in the paper, but nobody set a dog on him or hit him, and I had that happen."

"Right. Right, because we're more vulnerable," Lisa says.

"Or at least we are perceived that way," says Juanita. "But there are cases that hit closer to home for me, and I suspect, for other women. I remember in the federal defender's office, I got assigned to represent a man charged with raping and killing young Mexican women trying to cross the border. He worked as a guard. From a personal level, it was the first time I really had to grapple with how do I feel about — I'm not the one to judge whether he's guilty or not guilty, but if they're right and it's not just this woman, it's multiple women, if he's acquitted, he'll kill again. I'm being honest; I thought about it. It was disturbing to me. And especially as a young Hispanic woman, I could see myself right there. So I remember I called Garvin Isaacs — because Garvin had done some really tough cases like the Native American guy — what was his name — John Hart or something. A group of Girl Scouts were found raped and murdered in a tent out in Oklahoma at the campground. And this guy had been — his client had escaped from somewhere and was loose, and they thought for sure he had done it, and I think Garvin ended up getting him acquitted. So I remember calling Garvin because it was like a crisis of — not a crisis of faith, but do you know what I mean?"

"I sure do," says Cynthia Stewart. "You have to process this. It comes at some point, I think, in everybody's career, don't you?"

The Feminine Sixth: Women for the Defense

"Yeah. I would think so, or at least if you have — maybe it doesn't for everybody, but it did for me — because I thought, if I do my very best, which I'm supposed to do and I will do, and he's acquitted, he could kill again if he is truly a serial killer." Juanita pauses and swallows. "Not could, probably would. So I talked to Garvin, and basically Garvin said, 'That's not your job. Your job is to defend him with all your skills and talent, and your job is to keep the system honest and to make sure that they don't improperly stack the deck. You do all that and justice will be done one way or another.' And he may have not articulated just that — but whatever he said, I felt way better after that and I didn't think about it anymore. And I just did the very best that I could."

"Some defense lawyers decide there are certain cases they just can't do. Did you ever make such a decision? And if you did, how do you feel about having done so?" I ask.

"Well, I realized that child molestation cases weren't ones that I could do. I did one child molest case and I never did another one because the judge — this was in state court and back then, you did preliminary hearings. So the little girl testified while sitting on her mom's lap, and I was trying to see maybe it was transference that someone else had done this and she was saying it was her Uncle Bobby, and I actually got her to say that it actually had happened before, and I thought 'Ah.' And I said, 'Who was that?' And she says, 'Uncle Bobby.' I'm, like, 'Oh, God.' And I remember turning and thinking, 'You molested her twice? I'm going to kill you, you motherfucker,' which is not a good idea."

"Probably not. No."

"Probably screwed up," Juanita says with a sort of embarrassed half laugh. "I just knew this was not the right kind of case for me."

"I thought I would feel like that, but I have surprised myself," says Huma. "As a Muslim woman, raised in a modest way as I'm sure you can imagine, I had led a pretty sheltered life, and suddenly being plunged into the world of criminal defense, I was exposed to some of the darker aspects of humanity. So I don't want to say that I had a crisis of faith because it wasn't that, it was never that, and it's still not that. It's just that I was suddenly conscious of all the things I had never been exposed to. It did affect my religious practice because I found that the way that Islam was in my life and the way that my friends practiced it and school children practiced it, it was steeped in ritual and it was steeped in ideas of black-and-white: This is a sin, you will be damned to hell for it; this is a good deed, this is what you should do. Engaging with the world of criminal defense and seeing all the things that people do, people get caught up with, it just made me see that the vast majority of life is gray, it's not black-and-white. So that kind of informed how my religious practice changed a bit."

"Did you find that your parents didn't want you to do criminal defense or thought it was shameful?" I ask. "Especially since your firm does a lot of child pornography and other sexual offenses?"

"That was what happened at first. Exactly. But as I started working, my parents and particularly my father started seeing that that wasn't the reality of it. But he's still very proud of me. He always wants to have a stack of my cards on him; he gives them out to everyone. So he's very proud of the work I do, even though he knows that a lot of the things I deal with, write about, watch at work are things that he would never

The Feminine Sixth: Women for the Defense

ever consent to or want me to see or be exposed to my entire life. Even though he knows the conversations that I have with people of all ages and backgrounds involve words that he would never want me to say, for example. So, you know, all sorts of intimate things that his sense of decorum says that we shouldn't be talking about, especially young women shouldn't be talking about, shouldn't be aware of. So he still has that cultural traditional aspect of it, but he's still very, very proud of me for doing what I do, even though he knows it can be a bit raunchy and a bit out of his comfort zone for what he may have wanted me to do."

"Can you tell us a little bit about how you learned to deal with moral repugnance?" I ask.

"Well, when I started working for Wigell and Associates the first thing that I wrote for him was a motion in limine on a child pornography case where there had been child erotica — well, child pornography fan — well, narratives, stories about people having sex with children. They were found on our client's computer along with the contraband, and we obviously didn't want the jury to know about those if the case went to trial. So that was my first big motion. I didn't even know that child pornography existed at that point. I didn't know it was a thing that was out there in the world. I learned real quick that child pornography was there, some people were into it, and then they got charged with it. Our paralegal, too, was very protective of me the same way my boss was. So when she knew that Raymond had assigned me that motion, she said, 'Hon, you've never seen child pornography, you don't know what it is. We have some in our secure locker. Take a day, take some out, watch it. I'll watch it with you. If you need some time to process it, to cry, to throw up, whatever you want to do, do it, because the first time you see it or hear about it can't be in court.' So that was very helpful, how protective they both were of me."

"I noticed that when you started talking about how you never even knew child pornography was a thing, you were kind of smiling, and I couldn't tell if you were smiling kind of ruefully at yourself or what that smile was," I say.

"Well, I had led a very sheltered life, a very sheltered life, and part of it was my culture and my religion. Ever since a young age, my parents had decided there were certain things that were not to be discussed in front of me or with me. So when I was very young, it was money. My parents never discussed money in front of me. We were not well off, but I had no idea because they never, ever discussed any money troubles in front of me. I had no idea. Sex and anything related to that was definitely one of those things. They never discussed anything like that, they never let anything like that play on the television when I was in the room. So I had learned what sex was, but all of these other things, well, I just knew nothing about. But I have learned to handle it."

"Can you explain what you mean by 'handling' it?" asks Crystal.

"Sure," Huma continues. "Let's see. There was a client. He was a baseball coach and a paramedic in a kind of southern county in Illinois. It's a very rural county, one where I had never operated in other than this case, and he was accused of grooming and indecent solicitation of a minor. 'Grooming' is basically a series of — the way the state alleged — that it was a series of communications with the minor that were intended to kind of entice him into a romantic relationship. That was how the state phrased it. Then the indecent solicitation was actually the overt invitation to a sexual contact. This was a male student, so obviously there was the implication of our client being homosexual. We didn't trouble ourselves with that. It was just about what the state could show, all sorts of different things. During that process, I bonded very much with this client. It was a joy to talk to him on the phone, I found myself — anytime I filed a motion, I had to call him up and I would say, 'Hey, do you want a copy? Do you want to come pick it up? Do you want me to give it to you at the next meeting?' That client absolutely adored us."

"I didn't understand at the time why he loved us so much. From his perspective, anytime we did anything on the file, we told him. He felt very much in the loop and he loved us just for advocating for him that way. That was surprising to me because my perspective was I have to advocate for you this way. You're my client and this is the most natural thing in the world for me to do now that I've been taught what my duties are as a defense attorney. This client, there was nothing he could ask of me that was too onerous. Sometimes we rolled our eyes at little motions to expand the conditions of bond to allow out of state travel from Illinois to other places in the continental U.S. because they're a pain in the ass to do. If this client made a request, I had no problem with it. If he called me up kind of late at night, he was always very apologetic. But if he had a question, if some other emergency came up and he called me that was fine. It was a case that we took to trial and we ultimately lost, but getting to know him, to see him as a whole person not just some slimy headline, well that changed my perspective."

I turn to the audience. "I am wondering if any of you might like to ask the panelists any questions before we move on to our next subject?" I see some people moving to the microphones in the aisles. I nod to the first person to get to one. He is an older guy, with an actual scruffy beard instead of those ones that are cultivated. "Yes sir?" I ask.

"I wanted to follow up on Ms. Rashid's last comment about 'slimy headlines.' You have all talked about dealing with moral issues yourselves, but how does the media factor into all that?"

Lisa Wayne responds. "Well sometimes the added pressure of being in the news makes it that much harder to try a case. Remember the Hmong case I talked about earlier? Where it was clear we couldn't get a fair jury in Boulder, Colorado? The racism was so prevalent. We also tried to get the DA off of the case because I said she was running her election on the back of my case, and, of course, that didn't happen either. So we get a change of venue. And, as most places are, change of venues are random. You don't get to choose where you want to go. The chief judge of the Supreme Court assigns you, where they can take the case. So I got sent to the Western Slope to try this Hmong client. It was awful. It was a really ugly trial for two weeks. I was — felt very alone. So here I am in one of the hardest trials I'd ever done in my life and had at points — oh, and the paper had been going after me, by way, for going after the DA, so it was front-page news every single day. Every day." Lisa stops a moment. "So I was so overwhelmed that I did something stupid. I bounced a check. Of course no one knew it but me, but it was a return of funds to a client, and it caused all kinds of trouble for me." Lisa stops again. "What I am trying to say is that defending a 'bad' case is hard enough, it gets harder when you are being excoriated by the press and the public too."

The man looks as though he wants to ask something else, so I nod at him, but he shakes his head and takes his seat. I wonder what it was he wanted to ask, but then I look over at the other microphone, and there is this young woman standing there, looking very nervous. "You had a question?" I ask.

The Feminine Sixth: Women for the Defense

"Well, yes I do," she says. "I know you have talked about answering the 'how can you' question, but what about talking to your children or a close friend or family members' children about what you do, and who you represent?"

Cyndy Short answers, "Well, I can speak to that regarding my own children. The first instance with my first child, Kyle, is when he was — well, there were two events with Kyle, because when I went to Trial Lawyers College, Kyle was two, and I was gone for 30 days. And that's a long time to be away from a little guy like that. Then when he was three, I tried my death penalty case. So because of that, I was gone for a long time. And my husband was trying to explain to Kyle where I was. So Kyle was using language like 'Mommy's trying to save a man.' I think he must have utilized the word 'die,' because when it was finally over and I came home and they were in the basement and they came upstairs — I'll never forget this — Kyle looked at me startled, and he says to me in a worried way, 'Did the man die?' So somehow he had equated my coming home with the death of this man. So that, I think, was the moment where you realize the kids were going to be raised or have an awareness of things that would be different than other children. And then you had to start making decisions about how much and when you would expose them to what we were doing. But over the years, the kids have come to trials, I've had them come to sentencing hearings."

"I hear that," the questioner follows up. "But, what I mean is how do you 'defend' defending to a child?"

"You are making an assumption here," says Cynthia Roseberry. "The assumption that we do — or should — feel defensive about it." I see nods from other panelists. "If we feel that way some of the time — okay *when* we feel that way some of the time — is not when we have these conversations. We have them with the vulnerable audiences among those close to us when we are in a place where we are able to explain it well."

I watch the audience as this sinks in, and the young woman looks at Cynthia and there is suddenly a connection. I watch her hear Cynthia in a visceral way. Time to take a break, right now I think.

"Well I think it might be time to take a bit of a break, and when we come back we are going to discuss being a criminal defense lawyer and balancing that with the whole life we live." I smile and take a seat. This should be interesting.

CHAPTER FIVE:
LIFE/WORK BALANCE

I call things to order, and notice, with pleasure, that folks in the audience are talking to each other. Not chatting, really *talking*. I can't say how it is that I can tell the difference, but I can.

"Hi, everyone. We are going to start with the subject that is of a lot of interest to us all: life/work balance. I have to say the second most asked question I get — after 'how can you represent those people' — is about how I can be a criminal defense lawyer and still...fill in the blank: have children, a marriage, time for personal growth...all of those sorts of things. And I am very sure that this is not the question that men get asked often, if at all."

I look around as folks take their seats. My intention is to talk about personal lives, directly and in as much detail as my panelists would be comfortable with, and I tell the audience that.

Cynthia Roseberry speaks up. "Andrea, you have to do this too, you know. You are a 'first.'" She turns to the audience, "Did you know that Andrea Lyon was the first woman to be lead counsel defending a death penalty case in the country? Well she was and, I might add, she has won every death hearing she has ever done."

I could feel myself half way blushing. Not because it wasn't true, but because it was. "I worked hard, and had success, but I also had some luck," I say.

"Typical," chimes in Juanita. "This is one of our differences, gendered differences. Any guy would say it's because they are great."

"Maybe," says Cynthia Stewart, "but I know what you are saying."

"Do you think it's the extra chromosome?" asks Lisa.

"Can we get back to the subject?" I ask, trying not to laugh. "Let's talk about working as a criminal defense lawyer and trying to have personal lives too."

Juanita stands up. "Let me start with how I was told not to have a personal life when I started out in the San Diego Federal Defender's Office," she says. "It was a funny story. So, yeah, what was it like? It was amazing, intimidating, depressing, exhilarating. You know what I mean? Why do I say that? Because, first of all, John — my boss — taught you to be a wonderful lawyer. John Cleary, the chief, had certain rules. He had the 70-hour rule: You will work a minimum of 70 hours a week. Your clients have that right. He had the 24-hour rule: When a file hits your desk, you will be over in the jail seeing the client within 24 hours. You will never let someone sit over there for more than 24 hours before you see them. And he had the 500-foot rule, which was no fucking anybody that works within 500 feet of that flagpole. Meaning nobody in this office, because we were right across the street from the courthouse and there was a big flagpole in front of the courthouse, right?" Everyone is laughing by now. "So no

The Feminine Sixth: Women for the Defense

judge's clerks, no marshals, no U.S. attorneys, no probation officers. And then in our office, no staff, no attorneys, no investigators. Of course, nobody paid attention to *that* rule that John had." There is even more laughter.

"Of course, you wouldn't even be able to say such a thing now. But that was literally the 70-hour rule, the 24-hour rule, and the 500-foot rule. And he did use the 'F' word. Yes. And it was all men at that point because the one previous woman left. I was the only woman. And the guys were all really good lawyers, but they could have been on the legal version of 'Mad Men.' Some of them are still my really close friends, but they would drink every night and many of them were cheating on their wives with secretaries. Not all of them. May the record reflect I am not talking about every guy in the office, by any means. But, in other words, it was classic old guy — good old boy kind of mentality." Juanita pauses.

"And, as a result, pretty much impossible to have a relationship. So it was lonely when I wasn't working because I really didn't have time to make any friends or have a boyfriend or anything like that. So I remember going back to my apartment that was — I was still sleeping in a sleeping bag because I just didn't have time to get a bed or really very much money either. So I had a beach chair and a little black-and-white TV sitting on the floor in my living room. I had a sleeping bag and a foot locker for my clothes in the bedroom, and that's how my apartment was furnished."

"Wow," I say, remembering my one bedroom 'garden' apartment (read: basement with pipes running through open on the ceiling) that had been my first too.

"I remember Cleary was trying to get this one guy to come join the office and had me show him around for the day. Then I showed the guy my apartment because the guy — he asked, 'Could you show me places around here near the beach that are affordable if I did come to San Diego where I could live?' And I said, 'Oh, I live really near the beach and it's a really affordable place.' So I showed him my apartment. Then he ended up turning the job down. So Cleary said, do you know what he said to me? He said 'I went to her apartment; she's been here for a year and she still has no furniture. I don't want to live like that.'"

"So let's talk about marriage and children and having a personal and professional life," I encourage Juanita.

"Okay. Well, my first marriage lasted 18 years, a wonderful man, the father of my children, who is to this day a public defender with the Alternate Public Defender Association (an office for cases where there is a conflict), but I was always the breadwinner in the family, and it was always really clear. So I left federal defenders to open my own practice, so I'm kind of getting ahead of myself."

"When did you open your own practice?"

"I was at the federal defenders for three years and then decided to open up my own practice. And it turned out back then — I didn't even realize it — I was the only woman criminal defense lawyer that was not at a defenders office. I was the first one to hang out a shingle. I married really young. I was 24. We didn't have children right away because I was too focused on my career. So my daughter was born when I was 36, and then my son — we adopted him when I was 40. I didn't have my daughter until I was 36, so I think it was the classic biological clock. It never occurred to me to slow down long enough to have a child, working too hard, having to travel for work, at that point it started really growing. So I wasn't just getting referrals in San Diego, I was getting referrals around the country. And I just woke up one morning and said, 'I need to have a baby.' It's just that simple. I wish I could tell you a lot of thought went into it, but it didn't. I turned to my husband Bart. I'm like, 'Bart, I need to have a baby.' He's like, 'Well, I know how that could happen.' And then I was very fortunate because I had no issue getting pregnant. It was, like, first month, boom, that's it. Throw away the pills, have a baby. I know for everybody it's not that easy. It was for me."

"And that was another one where I'm glad I didn't know then what I had later learned, which is it never occurred to me how hard it was going to be, to continue — at that point I had my own practice still — to continue to run my own practice and be a mom. I made no plans for once the baby was born, what I was going to do. I tried two cases while I was pregnant out of town, one in town and two out of town, in San Francisco, one when I was seven months pregnant. I would get on the flight — I would fly home on the weekends. I would get on the flight to go back up to San Francisco on Sunday night, and that flight went on to Seattle. And each time the flight attendants would be, 'You're not going all the way to Seattle, are you?' because they were afraid I might not make it. I made no plan. Rose ended up being born a month early because I had gone full out, and my OB/GYN said, 'You're never going to carry this baby full term.' I said, 'Look, I've got to work as far as I can.'"

"So I planned to block out a month when Rose was born. She was supposed to be born in mid-August, so from mid-August to mid-September I kind of blocked out. But mid-July to mid-August was jammed with stuff, and she was born on July 21st, and I had to be back in court, like, three days later. So it was that part I hadn't really thought about. And, luckily, I had a client whose wife had a small child and had this network of British nannies. And so she said to me, 'I'm going to set you up with a nanny because obviously you've not thought about this.'"

I start to laugh — this sounds so familiar in so many ways — I also was 36 when I had my daughter. The audience is chuckling too at Juanita's description.

"I'm like, 'No, I really haven't.' Thank goodness that I had a really good nanny right out of the box or I don't know what would have happened."

I respond, "Some women make a decision not to have children who do this work for all different kinds of reasons. Had that ever occurred to you that you wouldn't, or was it just sort of an unspoken assumption?"

"I'd never really thought about it, to be honest," answers Juanita. "I've never said to myself, 'Oh, this life does not fit with having a child.' I didn't say that, I didn't say — yes, I didn't say no. I just didn't think about it. I just kind of kept one foot in front of the other until I woke up one morning and said, 'I want to have a baby.' And at this stage, I really counsel the women that I work with, the young women, that you can do it. You can have career and you can have children, and don't feel like you have to give up either one of those. That is so wrong and that is so depriving yourself of either one."

"Now, some women don't have children because they don't want children, but they shouldn't not have children because they want a career and they think it's binary. It's like, 'If I'm going to have a child, I can't have a career; if I'm going to have a career, I can't have a child.' It shouldn't be that way. So I really, really encourage these young women that you can do both."

"I gave a talk once with a couple of other women about this, the whole work/life balance thing, and one of the women had the best line. She said, 'You know what? If, on any given day, I'm not failing, I'm getting a 'C' as a wife, a mother, and a lawyer, that's a good day. If I'm not flunking one of the big '3s,' that's a good day.' So you don't have to get straight A's. There will be times when you're getting straight A's in your career and you're getting a C-minus as a mom, and there will be times when you're getting straight A's as a mom and you might be getting a C-minus as a wife or whatever. And you learn little tricks."

"To this day, my friend Kelly, who was about to quit my law firm because she had two little kids and she just thought, this is not going to work, luckily I was her kind of mentor at that point. I gave her some tips. I said, 'Alright. Here's the first thing: frozen cookie dough.' She's like, 'What?' I said, 'Frozen cookie dough. Here's why: Because your child is going to say to you at 11:00 o'clock at night, 'Mom, I'm supposed to bring cookies for the 30 kids in my class tomorrow morning.'" Everyone is laughing now.

"Yes. Yes, she is." Why hadn't I thought of that?

"And they will not tell you that until 11:00 o'clock the night before. And if you've got the frozen cookie dough, you go, 'Okay. That's fine.' You cut up the cookie dough, you put it in the oven, and there's your fresh cookies. So you don't go running out to the grocery store; you have your frozen cookie dough. That's number one. Number two, good help. It's really important and don't skimp on it. If it means don't get your nails done, don't go out to dinners to get that money to hire someone you really trust to be with your child when you cannot, that's where you put your money. And number three is the 'Three C' rule. It's okay to be doing an okay job, not to get straight A's every day, all the time, in every category. I had my son Jai at that point who was two years old when Bart and I divorced."

I ask Juanita, "So after you and Bart separated, did that coincide with your sort of leaving criminal defense? Did you actually make a conscious decision to leave it?"

"Yes and no, which is the lawyer answer, right? It's like a fricking lawyer answer. Well, one that I think that happened was that in — well, Jai was just here, so '94, '95, I got involved in this Medicare fraud case. I wasn't supposed to be lead counsel, I was supposed to just help. 'Racehorse' Haynes was counsel for this doctor who was charged with this massive Medicare fraud where he supposedly was telling elderly people that they had cataracts when they didn't and then doing cataract surgery on someone who didn't have cataracts and supposedly doing other medically unnecessary procedures for the money. That was the allegation and it was a massive, massive case. But 'Racehorse' was supposed to be lead trial counsel; I was just supposed to help out and I am not sure, but I think I felt at the time that doing criminal defense negatively impacted my life, and I needed to make more money too."

"Do you think that it was criminal defense that affected your relationship? Lawyering? Both?"

"I think it was lawyering. I don't think it was the criminal defense, per se. I could see where it would if you allowed yourself to become bitter, angry, jaded. That, I could get. But if it's just the long hours, I put in just as long hours now as I did as a criminal defense lawyer, and I get just as preoccupied

The Feminine Sixth: Women for the Defense

and absorbed and distracted. It's just that if I have a loss, I get over it quicker. So maybe an upside is I don't sit around for a month or two months eating my guts out anymore. But, no, I don't think that's what it was. The long hours, sure, but not criminal defense, per se, although I could see it in some of my colleagues who would drink too much to drown out. Sometimes you see too much."

"Well I know what a long trial can do," I comment. "I remember after a month-long welfare fraud jury trial ended, well somewhere in that month I lost a boyfriend somewhere. I don't know what happened to him; he just kind of disappeared." Juanita laughs. So does the audience.

"Cynthia?" I say to Cynthia Roseberry. "Can you talk a little about work and life and love?"

"Is that all?" she quips. "My first husband was Rick Jones. He's from Indianapolis, Indiana. His best friend has a brother who is married to a first cousin I found out about after meeting him. But he was in the ROTC program and we married. He was being sent to Germany, so we got married. I went to Germany and lived there with him for three years. We divorced shortly after that."

"When you lived in Germany, how old were you? Were you through college at that point?" I ask.

"I was done with college; I was 21, got chicken pox in Germany, which was an interesting experience because I quickly learned the word for 'chicken' in German is 'hahnchen,' and the word for 'pox' is 'pocken.' So I remember telling a neighbor of mine, 'Ich habe Hahnchen pocken.' Well, there's a German word for 'chicken pox,' it's 'windpocken.' So I clearly told the woman, 'I have chicken disease.'" She laughs. "We stayed married seven years, but three, we lived together for three."

"And did you ever talk about having a family or anything, or was that just not in the cards?"

"He wanted to start a family there and I wasn't ready because actually, when I was there, I looked into going to law school. There was one English-speaking law school in Germany, and I could go for two weekends a month to study. But it was a considerable distance away and I was really frightened to drive in the snow and the ice. It was really scary to me as a southerner, and especially there. So I didn't go. But I wanted to go to law school before having children. I thought I should do that, so we didn't have kids. My second husband was Horace Roseberry. We met at a party, and he came up and said something to me. We just started dating, and we dated for about a year. His family's actually from Washington, D.C., but he had lived in Atlanta and went to Morehouse, kind of like my father. On leap year, February 29th, on a leap year, I asked him to marry me."

"You did?"

"I did." Cynthia's dimples are flashing.

"Well, we all want to know more!" I say laughing. I see smiles in the audience and on the panel.

"Well, I was joking and he took it seriously, and I couldn't back down. I asked him, I said, 'It's leap year. You know, the woman asks. Will you marry me?' And he goes, 'Yeah.' And so I didn't think anything of it. We were still dating, and months later he asked me if I had started planning the wedding. And I said, 'What wedding?' And he said, 'You asked me to marry you.'

The Feminine Sixth: Women for the Defense

And so I thought, well, he's nice enough and he's handsome, and I'm, like, 'Yeah. Well, okay. We'll get married.' And by the time we decided to get married, my sister won the lottery. And although I asked — she wanted to do something for me; I asked her if she would pay my student loans, and she said no, but she would do a wedding. So we had a wedding where? At the High Museum of Art in Atlanta, of course. It was a nice wedding. He delivered packages for Federal Express, but he had a license to be an aircraft mechanic, so he switched over to Delta Airlines and started working on their airplanes. That's what he still does now, and he teaches at the school there as well. We lived happily for three years and we were married for seven, and then divorced. He's a nice guy."

"Let's talk a bit about work/life balance, if that's okay. Your two marriages that were good for three years and then ended after seven, which seems to be your magic number." Cynthia nods and laughs good-naturedly. "Do you think it's hard for a woman to have a life, to have children, to have a husband or a girlfriend or whatever, and do this work?"

"Let me answer that this way. I can remember a couple of stories from being married to Horace Roseberry because that's when I was a lawyer, right? The first is on our first date, he made dinner for me. And I can remember into the marriage when I was building a practice and I had to come home late because you have to do court in the day and client visits at night. I mean, that's what you have to do. I came home late one night, and I remember he was sitting at the dinner table with an empty plate and knife and fork, and he said he was waiting for me to make his dinner. And something just washed over me. I thought, I could never do that as a woman, right, saying, 'I'm waiting for you to make me dinner,' despite the fact that he cooked for me on our first date to impress me with his cooking. But he just needed for me to fit into that traditional role. He would ask me why I couldn't be a corporate lawyer; why did I have to work and go into the jails, and why did I have to do that kind of work? There were so many men in that work; why did I have to be around that work and why did I have to work so many hours? Why did I care about those criminals? Why would you care about them? They're knuckleheads, you know. And he just thought it was more ladylike for me to put on a suit and work 9:00 to 5:00 in some corporation as a lawyer. Of course, I absolutely had no passion for that, and that was the source of a lot of tension in the marriage. We didn't have children. I was happy that we didn't, frankly, because I just don't think I could have managed that. If he's sitting at home, waiting for me to make dinner, then surely he would be upset if I was missing a play for a child or what have you, right? That would have been a problem."

I start to ask another question, but Cynthia continues, "Whatever reward you get from it is going to have to come from you, from your heart. And if your heart is in it, you should. It's going to be tough and you're going to deal with things that male lawyers don't have to deal with, but you can find great reward in it. But I want to encourage balance. This is what a judge told me years ago: Don't look back after 20 years and all you've done is work. And it's easy to do because you get so engrossed in the work. Try to find something else in life that brings you joy and pleasure and a sense of fulfillment at the same time, because there are a number of alcoholics in our profession, there are a number of people who are divorced. We have a lot of mental illness in our profession. One of my good friends, who was a tremendous lawyer, shot himself dead in the parking lot of the Georgia Bar, the Bar Association building. So you have to make sure you have some balance in this. Search your heart, and if your heart is in it, you should definitely do it." All of the panelists are thinking about this — we all know someone in our line of work who has killed themselves. I found myself thinking of my late friend Bill Bryson from Alaska. He shot himself.

"Have any of you ever talked to any of your mentees or younger colleagues about trying to do that for themselves, to make sure that they keep time, some time, for themselves?" I ask.

Crystal Marchigiani speaks up. "Yes. They're different. The younger lawyers in the office, a lot of the younger women lawyers in the office, they made the choice to be more family oriented, so they actually — one might think you might want to tell them to spend more time at work. The problem is the opposite balance maybe, you know? And there was a time — and I remember my friend Debbie White and me talking about this. She was chief of Felony Trial Division while I was chief of Homicide Task Force, and a lot of the lawyers in her division were seeking to be promoted to Task Force. But she had a funny conversation with several of them separately. They would come into her office, these young women, and they would say, 'But look at all the single women in Task Force; I don't want to be like that.' And she was right. There are a lot of single women in Task Force. There are a lot of single, 40-year-old women in Task Force, and it's just a fact and I don't know what the reason is. But I'll bet the reason is work-life balance isn't easy."

"What about you? How did you manage love in your life? Maybe starting with law school?" I ask Crystal.

"Well, let's be honest. When I was in law school there were some people that I went to dinner with because I was really poor and really needed to eat, so I dated." There is a ripple of laughter in the room. "But I was also crazy in love with a guy that I had met in Santa Clara. He was an engineer and he was working, but he was in his first years of working. So while he would come to San Francisco, you know, he was in San Jose, he was in Gilroy, California, he was in Sacramento during part of that time. He was moving around because he was new to his career. And while he would take me out and all that kind of stuff when he was in town, he wasn't always in town. So I was crazy in love with him, and we moved in together in San Jose for a while. And at that point, I was working in the Santa Clara County public defender's office. We were together through law school and the first part of my working in San Jose. I think I always expected to get out of law school and go to work with my parents' friend Douglas, and then I didn't because I met the public defender's office, and that's a calling. And when you are right for the public defender's office, that's all you want to do, and that's what I wanted to do."

"I was living with that boyfriend, and things didn't work," Crystal continues. "You know what happened? My first jury trial, it was a woman client; I adored her. She was charged with criminal damage to — it seems silly now — she was charged with criminal damage to a jail cell, so she was drunk and disorderly and punching holes in the jail wall or whatever, you know, people did at that time. And I really wanted to win her case. And my jury trial was set for the next day and it was the first jury ever for me, first jury I had been involved in. We didn't have partners in that office. We tried our cases ourselves. So it's just me, and I'm going into a jury trial the next day. And I was nervous and all those things. I was not just anxious, I was beyond anxious with a client I really cared about. And I didn't know what I was doing. My boyfriend invited his entire family over for dinner to celebrate my next-day jury trial — I just thought to myself that he is never going to understand. He is never going to understand. So it was kind of the beginning of the end. It wasn't the end, but it was the first time I ever thought or had to think, oh, my God, what if the other in your life doesn't understand what you're

The Feminine Sixth: Women for the Defense

doing? You know, because it was the first time I had been doing anything like that. So it was sort of the beginning of the end. Then I met my husband Dan and moved to Chicago and joined the public defender's office here."

"You didn't have children, is that right?" I ask. "Was that a conscious decision not to have children?"

"No. No. And I don't really know how I feel about it. But what happened was I moved here; I was almost 30 when I got married, and I don't think Dan nor I ever thought we wouldn't have children, and I'm quite sure that my mother-in-law thought I was her best hope at grandchildren. But here's what happened: I felt like I needed to make a name for myself in the office. I had been — in my own opinion — I had been on the rise in the Santa Clara office, and people knew who I was. To say that that wasn't true here was not putting it strongly enough. I mean, I didn't have any connections. I hadn't gone to law school here, I didn't know any judges, nobody knew who I was, and I wanted to be in the Task Force, and I knew I had to come to the attention of people. So I knew that I had to put having kids on a back burner, and I didn't think anything of it at the time. And then when I was — I was probably 34 when I was promoted to Task Force, close to 34, maybe a little more, maybe a little less, when I was promoted to Task Force, and I kind of thought that would be the time, but that was the time when the doctors told me that that was not going to happen."

"I am so sorry," Cyndy Short says. There is a quietness in the audience too. This is painful.

I wait a moment. "I do still want to ask you a little bit about work/life balance, if that is okay?" She nods.

"I have been very careful to protect time with Dan, to set it aside. Since the beginning of our marriage, so 30 years ago this year, we have always gone out to dinner on Friday nights. When I first married Dan, he opened the shop on Saturdays for half a day, and that was always — Saturday morning when he was at the shop was kind of my time for all of that stuff that we bring home to do, the reading, the end writing of the motion, all that stuff, police reports that you can read at home. And that worked pretty well. But then I began to think, you know, how fun is this for him to realize that all of this intensity and all of this time away is because I'm completely focused on somebody that isn't him, and how would I feel if that was his life? So I don't know how two lawyers do it together. But I remember this: He was talking to me about something, and I don't know that it was really a fight, but it might have been an argument. And being in the middle of this death penalty case, and turning to him and saying, 'Are we going to get divorced over this? Because if we're not going to get divorced over this, I have to talk about it at some other time.' When I recounted this story to my colleagues at work, they were all, like, 'Oh, my God, how could you have said that?' But at the time it worked completely, because he said, 'No, we're not getting divorced about this, but we are going to talk about it later.' And that was fine. 'I can talk about it later; I just can't talk about it now. I can talk about it if we're going to get divorced over it because you're more important to me than that.' You know what I mean?"

"I know what you mean," says Cynthia Stewart. "I loved gardening and it has helped me with that balance in my rather fraught personal life."

"Gardening?"

143

The Feminine Sixth: Women for the Defense

She nods firmly. "Yes, gardening. Yes. My father, to humor me as much as anything, built me these large boxes. He farmed a little bit. He was kind of the generation where if you got a couple of cows and a garden, you might be okay. He grew up in the depression. He had his big garden and they all grew up — children worked back then. But he made these boxes for me and filled them with dirt, and this is before the concept of box gardening or mound gardening had come into vogue. He just did it to kind of give me a place to grow what I wanted to grow. I grew herbs, and he had a friend at ATF that would come out and would bring me these unusual herbs, and I would grow them and figure out ways to use them, and we'd read books on how they could be used medicinally. I still do that a little bit. All over my yards I have different herbs planted. I would have to have more time to pay attention to that. I like to cook, I'm a good cook when I want to. I'm an unreliable cook if you expect it to happen every day."

"Tell me about your balance of life and work. Do you have children?"

Cynthia Stewart smiles and shakes her head. "Yes, but I didn't do pregnancies very well. Neither of them."

"You were ill?"

"I was ill the whole time. I threw up and threw up and threw up and threw up."

"And then you did it again?"

"Well, keep in mind that I waited 12 years." There is laughter.

"Okay. I will keep that in mind. Tell me about marriage?"

"You mean marriages? Well I married my first husband who is older than I was by about eight years, and he came to teach; he had his master's in architecture at that point, and he came to teach. Mississippi State has an architecture program, and at that particular time — it didn't last long — but they brought the fifth-year architecture students to Jackson to complete their degree at that A&D Center there that serves Mississippi universities. I met him at the Unitarian church. We had an extremely amicable divorce. My girls all considered — he remarried and had two boys. They call my girls their sisters; all of my girls call them their brothers, and he married a woman that, unlike me and most people I know, I don't think has a mean bone in her body. She's a wonderful person. He seems happy."

"You do, too, actually."

"Eh, I'm quietly miserable." Cynthia laughs.

"So the first couple of years of the marriage were pretty good. Tell me about your children."

"Well, I had graduated in 1983, I was working for the United League of Holmes County. We decided to have a baby, and at some point, I don't know how far along, it probably wasn't very, they kept writing me prescriptions, which I kept not taking because I was so scared to take them, but I was throwing up all the time. All day, every day, and I had to take an extra year off after she was born. That was the only time I've ever taken off with any of my children. And I believe that — it's probably not politically correct or popular, but I do believe when women take off and their husband becomes the sole financial supporter that it has a bad effect on the marriage, except I think the baby needs that first year."

The Feminine Sixth: Women for the Defense

"Well not everyone can or wishes to make that choice," says Juanita.

"That's true," Cynthia responds. "I couldn't do that with my second child because from the ages of 2 to 5, she was a fit-throwing demon from hell." There is widespread laughter.

"I can remember thinking at one point that — I remember coming home when Ann Gabriel was a babe, and she was all over me, 'Mama, Mama, Mama, Mama,' and I was just dead tired. I remember sitting down at some point and thinking it through and thinking that I have two jobs, and the second is really more important than the first. And once I thought — I know that's a terrible thing to say about motherhood — but once I regarded it as a case, but I'm now on this job, then I found ways to deal with it. I said, 'Ann Gabriel, I need five minutes, and then we're good to go.' She'd give me that five minutes and we were good to go. But I also remember thinking — and I'm not sure that there's not some truth to this — I remember thinking, 'I can be a very good lawyer and raise these children and be a good mother, but I can't be a good mother and be a truly great lawyer.'"

"Why do you say that?"

"Because children need my presence, and during, for example, two weeks in January and really for several weeks leading up to that, I was in absentee mode. My daughter didn't, and my home didn't, see a lot of me, and that's hard on her. At one point when I just had Ann Gabriel, I would have to go get work, so I had to go up to Georgia, Tennessee, and Texas, surrounding states, maybe Alabama. I'm not sure that it ever got to the point where I had to enter an appearance. That was out. When I just had Ann Gabriel, I would go to other cities frequently and travel. I tried it both ways, but I found that bringing my family with me, I felt pulled in two different directions, when I should be downstairs networking and meeting people, and I can't just park my husband as the babysitter. It was better not to take them along. I'm just now to the point where I can resume some of that and I'm trying to put that in place. That might not have been as true with Laura Grace having had the problems that she had. That involved a lot of time. The courts were extremely accommodating and didn't have — maybe one judge would give me difficulty about something that had to be moved. Some things kind of became cemented in my mind, one of those being that no woman should ever have more children than she herself can take care of."

"Why did that become important to you?"

"I guess between reading it and looking around — I suppose even then I had a pretty strong maternal streak. And by that, I don't mean that I liked a bunch of other people's children; I mean that I'm very maternal for all of them and my extra girls. And I thought I have to be able to take care of them. You know, ultimately it's my responsibility for this."

"That seems to be a pretty clear feeling we all share. What do you think Lisa?" I ask.

"Well, things are complicated regarding who takes responsibility for what. I think there are many ways in which being as strong as you need to be to do this work can be challenging. Sometimes you have to say that you can't think about all that, you just have to let it go. For example, go and find the guy or woman who is 100 percent supportive of you, not intimidated by you, and not threatened by that ego because trial lawyers have immense egos and that is a very hard one to reconcile in a relationship. You know, that's not always a plus. So it's a balance. I think you see it, Andrea.

The Feminine Sixth: Women for the Defense

You see a lot of your very tough, strong women friends, and they can become kind of passive in their relationships where they kind of let their men lead, but their relationships seem to be very successful and long-standing. I've always thought maybe that's why I can't do it, because they can give up what I'm unable to give up and let them lead. That leading thing is a tough one for me. I think maybe I'd be happier if I would let him lead. But that's a tough call, letting them lead. My mom says that all the time."

"I am sure you are not the only one to have heard that." I look around at the panel, there are nods. There are nods in the audience too. "You have one son, right? Tell us about that?"

"When I got pregnant with Dylan, I was in Colorado. My brother was in Florida at the time, my sister lived in Florida, and my parents lived in California. It's interesting. I got pregnant; my dad said, 'We're retiring and we're moving to help take care of Dylan,' because nobody ever thought I would have a kid. So they were, like, 'We're coming home.' So they moved back to Colorado, to Golden. My dad retired from the job he was in, which was the vice chancellor of students at Sac State in California, Sacramento State, and came back to Denver, and my sister shortly thereafter moved back to Denver, and my brother left the company that he was at, not because of me; he got a better job offer, and came to Colorado Springs. So ultimately we all ended up back in Colorado."

"So that's the effect your starting a family had on your family?" We both laugh.

"I know. It's so funny. I was, 'Really? Is it that startling?'"

"As we have been hearing, having a personal life at all is pretty difficult doing this work for many women. Can we just talk about that a little bit?"

"I don't think having a personal life is difficult. The problem is it's isolated. When I said we only date ourselves and we're very incestuous, it's because your life, particularly as a public defender, you work so much. You breathe it, you work it, you live it, and your clients are on your mind constantly. So nobody really wants to deal with that with you other than your colleagues. So I dated a lot of public defenders. Those are the people that I dated, the people I lived with for a very long time, a public defender. My ex-husband was a public defender at the time when we got pregnant and had Dylan. So that was my life in terms of my social life, my best friends. I was in a very big office, so I think if you were in a rural county, it would play very differently. But I was in Denver and I was okay with that, I was good, because, frankly, those are the people that could relate to me as well. We all had a lot of the same political ideals and we all had the same kind of aspirations. So that part was okay for me, I guess. I got divorced, so maybe it wasn't so great. Maybe I could have met a life partner if he hadn't been a public defender. I don't know. I don't have regrets like that. I don't think about 'what if,' or 'it could have been.' I'm very happy with the way that things went, even the heartbreak parts. So I just don't like to live like that, live my life like that. I could see where it might be difficult, though, depending upon where you are."

"Did you feel supported by your colleagues?" asks Amanda.

"There were detractors. There were things that happened in hindsight that I see that were different for me as a woman because, first of all, I was a single mom and there was a lot of traveling that had to go on. Dylan was a junior in high school.

The Feminine Sixth: Women for the Defense

I think he was a junior or senior. I can't remember. But there were times I just couldn't be on the road all the time. The men that are presidents or have been presidents either have wives at home taking care of the kids — none of them are raising kids. There's not a single dad that has been a president, okay? So I couldn't give — I had to be around for Dylan and I made a promise that I wasn't going to let it interfere. So I didn't get to travel as much and I didn't get to go on the Hill as much. I wasn't on the East Coast; I was in Colorado. So jumping on that plane to be in DC or New York for something when I was president of the National Association of Criminal Defense Lawyers, I couldn't do just like that. So that worked to my disadvantage. I noticed that. The women presidents other than me, Judy Clarke didn't have kids, Nancy Hollander didn't have kids, Barbara Bergman didn't have kids, Cynthia Orr didn't have kids, and Carmen Hernandez had a grown daughter and a husband at home. So that was a huge difference for me."

"Do you consider yourself a mentor or role model?" I ask.

"Not so much. It doesn't mean I don't have this great sense of mentoring and pride in the women thing, and I've been a huge female mentor because it is important. But it's not my focus in terms of what I carry on my shoulders. But the staying healthy thing is really a big deal for us. We just have a tendency to forget about it because we're taking care of everybody else, including our felonies, and we come last. When I got so ill, yoga saved my life. I think it did. I was a runner and I had to stop running. Yoga has really saved my life because it makes you force yourself to this meditation and mindfulness, and it sounds so hokey, but there's a reason it's been around so long. The reason is that it works. So that's huge. I think being soft, losing softness. And that's my mother's comment about the femininity. I do think you lose a softness. I don't know if that's good or bad. I don't know if there's anything wrong with it or not. I do sometimes catch myself just thinking, don't be so harsh, not judgmental, but just harsh, about my sense of what's right in the world. Well, I guess that is judgmental. I feel that for women, it's tougher. For men, it's looked on as that's a great characteristic, that's a positive characteristic. For us it's looked on as a negative; she's kind of egotistical, she's too confident."

"Do you find that you can get that from other women — I don't mean romantically — too?" asks Amanda. "With those who can become your work partners and close friends?"

"It can," says Lisa.

"After all," Amanda continues, "your work partnerships are a part of your life too."

"They are." I agree. "Perhaps I could bring up a subject that is both a good and a bad one, which is your very close friendship and ultimate partnership, at least for a time, with Katie Kizer, who was also a DePaul (and my) student. Would you mind talking about that a little, Amanda?"

"No, not at all. So it was probably the summer between the second and third year of law school. Katie and I had met within the first few days of law school and it was like we had known each other for years. We clicked. We got a lot done together and tried to make things fun as much as you can when you're taking Civil Procedure and Torts. Then by the time it came for us to take criminal law, we both really, really liked it, and I told her, 'I'm going to be applying to Andrea's clinic; you might want to consider it, and here's some information about Andrea in case you need any more convincing,' and I think she was immediately excited about that. So we worked in the clinic together, we worked with you together, so we both kind

The Feminine Sixth: Women for the Defense

of had a similar approach to doing criminal defense work. We also did a summer internship together, and so we got to get some real experience under our belts between the clinic and having our 711, or student in court, licenses in the public defender's office. So we came to the conclusion with you that — I remember we were walking on the beach with you, working on something, and you really empower us — it was a thought that was in our minds, the idea of starting our own practice, but you really said, 'I think you should do it.' You were so encouraging. Unfortunately Katie became ill, and I continued on by myself for a while before being lucky enough to get my dream job at the federal defender's office."

"Can you speak to the work/life balance question that we are discussing?" I ask.

"Yeah. I think I'm still figuring this one out, and I don't know if there's ever going to be a day when I feel like I know the answer to this question, because I think it's one of those things that you have to take day by day. I think it's very hard on the whole to say whether you can have both. I think I try to ask myself every day what I'm going to do for myself, and I think putting pressure on myself to say, you know, for the next two years what am I going to do for myself, or for the next ten years, but every day, and just take it one day at a time. The work will always be there the following day. So I never really have to ask that question: What am I going to do for work today? That will always be there. I think I do try to be more conscious of what I'm going to do for myself."

"When you say that, could you give me an example of what you mean?"

"Sometimes it means just taking care of myself like going to yoga or getting a manicure; other times I think it's being sure to set aside time for my partner, spend time with our pets. You know, I have a lot of respect for women who have kids amidst some really intense criminal defense work. I have friends who have done that. I asked one friend — Sarah Gelsomino from People's Law Office about it. She recently had her third child and then just three weeks later, I think, maybe a little more, went to trial on that Illinois terrorism case and won. I asked her afterwards, 'How in the hell did you do that?' I feel stressed at the idea of that kind of trial by itself, let alone having three kids, one of whom is depending on me for food. And she said, 'I don't know how else to explain it other than when you become a mom, you get super powers.'"

"Well, I don't know about that," I respond, "But I did have quite a winning streak when I was pregnant — even when it didn't show." We smile.

"Christine," I ask, "Can you talk about some of these same issues with us? I think you mentioned getting looked at as being not so bright since you are young and pretty — my words not yours."

"Um-hum. I think the number of times people have commented on the way I look, I try to just reflect and think, okay, maybe that's normal. But then I think about if I was a guy. Even if I was a young good-looking guy, I just don't think it would happen with the frequency it happens. And it's in the context where you should be talking about someone's liberty, but instead, that becomes something of a topic of conversation and I just." She sighs, "I get really upset about it."

"How about life/work balance? Do you see yourself being able to manage that as a criminal defense lawyer?"

The Feminine Sixth: Women for the Defense

"I am not sure. Here I am, oh, I'm in the Bay Area, I'm a public defender, and this is exactly where I want to be. And then I'm just, is this it? Is this what I'm going to do forever? I was talking to one of my colleagues, who is a senior public defender, does a bunch of the murder cases. He has fairly young children. He was talking about a case where he was thinking about — well, he was changing his kid's diaper or something like that, and he was thinking about while he was changing his kid's diaper what his opening statement was going to be like. While he's changing his kid's diaper, he just — it was very nonchalant. It wasn't like he was emphasizing that I just knew the context. I think he was telling me the ideas that were developing for his opening statement as he was changing his kid's diaper. And I just paused and I was, like, I don't want to do that. When I'm changing my kid's diaper, I want to change my kid's diaper. I don't want to be worried about what I'm going to say because I have to make sure that my client doesn't go to prison for the rest of his life, and be worried and stressed out about that."

"And it kind of clicked for me in that way. I was, like, can I do this? Do I want to do this forever? If I have a little girl or a little boy and they have Little League or they have this or they have that, but I have a life case going on and I have to work on that night instead of watching the recital or something like that." She pauses, her brow furrowed in concentration. "And I was, like, oh, my gosh, do you have to choose? Because you know what I'm going to choose: I'm going to choose my client. And it was, wow, that was really powerful for me to think that because I hadn't thought that way before. I'm thinking, you know, I'm going to choose my client over my kid. Holy shit. Do I want to put myself in that position once I get to that level? And I started thinking that maybe I don't want to be a public defender forever after that. So I started just to explore what else interested me, and coaching was really interesting, I'm still doing that."

"So you are sure you want to have children?" I ask.

"I always grew up thinking and knowing that I want to be a mom. I've been through different phases in my life where I remember just a few years ago where I thought, 'Oh, if I don't marry someone, if I don't find right partner, I'm probably just going to have my own kid.' Maybe I'll get a donor, maybe I'll find someone, maybe I'll adopt. I don't know. But I want to raise a child, I want to raise another human being. I want to help foster the growth of someone and help them to be who it is they want to be and just create more goodness in the world. That was like this whole idea I had, like, okay, if I don't find the right partner, I'm going to just have a kid. Then I realized that that wasn't as important to me. What was more important and what I really wanted was to raise a family with someone — that I don't want to raise a child as a single mother that I actually want to have a partner and raise a child together. I wanted to raise a family, not a person. I still feel that way now."

"But because I'm 32 and a lot of my friends are either married and have kids, engaged and getting married, I don't see myself in them, in the space of their life right now. I don't know that that has to do with the nature of my work. I don't think it does. I think it has more to do with just who I am as a person, but I'm not sure. I'm still trying to figure out why it is that the more my friends and the more the people around me — even my younger sister, she just got engaged and she's a few years younger than me, and I'm really happy and excited for her. So I guess what I'm trying to say is I don't really know where I'm at right now. I know that the more everyone else around me is quote, unquote, 'settling down,' the less I want it for myself."

The Feminine Sixth: Women for the Defense

"Huma do you feel the same?" I ask. "Now that you're the ripe old age of 29, whether you can date, whether — you're still living at home?"

"I am," Huma smiles. "I've lived at home all of my life. It's a very strong cultural expectation and a decision on my part. Most of my friends in high school, for example, the understanding was when they left to go to college, once they graduated college, they would be expected to find their own place to live, if not already having done that. But for me, that was never the case. The expectation in our culture is girls especially live at home until they get married. The boys can move out and do what they want, but the expectation is that the girls live at home until they get married."

"My parents are not as traditional as a lot of Muslim and South Asian parents in that regard, but they're certainly more traditional than a lot of other Muslim parents and South Asian parents. So it's a huge spectrum. I had Muslim friends who were women who moved out and got their own apartment and their parents were accepting of it, and I have friends who absolutely are not leaving the house until they get married. It was something I knew, that if I moved out, my parents would take it very badly, so I never did because I didn't want to have that confrontation. I didn't want to upset them that way, and it wasn't worth it at that time to me. I've been approaching the point where it is worth it. It's worth moving out, it's worth having that confrontation, that discussion, because I can't stay stagnant that way much longer, especially given the location of the firm. A lot of my work is downtown. It makes way more sense — I would love to be living in the city and being a part of Chicago." She shakes her head.

"I am not sure about how to have a personal life, or how to balance that with my work." She grins, "That was going to be your next question, right?" I nod.

"I don't want you to think I have no personal life. I have always been blessed with wonderful friends. I have friends that I've known since I was — my goodness — ten. One of my best friends I met when I was ten at my private Islamic school. She's married now, she lives in Canada, but every time she comes back, it's like she never left. My friends in high school, some of my closest friends are my friends that I met in high school, and I've been at their weddings, and those that still live here, we still hang out regularly and I know what's going on in their lives, they know what's going on in mine. My best friend is someone that I met my first day of law school, and I was part of his wedding and we see each other probably every week, we talk every day. So I'm very blessed with a nice circle of what I think of as chosen family. That's always been very important to me because I know that, for example, if I want to vent, there are friends I can go do that to. If I want to just hang out and let loose a bit, there are friends like that as well. So they're a very good source of support. As far as dating, that has been interesting just because I have never been much of a success when it comes to men, just never, and that hasn't changed much, I don't see it changing. I don't really know why it's the situation, but it is."

"When you say you haven't been much of a success, it sounds like you're taking this in on yourself, like there's something wrong with you. Am I hearing that correctly, or no?"

"It's quite possible. It's a conclusion that I think I've drawn based on my experience. Whether it's fair to me or not, I don't know. But that's just the conclusion I seem to have drawn. I've no shortage of male friends, to the point that I

The Feminine Sixth: Women for the Defense

sometimes try to be more conscious about spending more time with my female friends or making more friends with women or nurturing those relationships a bit more because they are different even though they are both lovely. But as far as anything beyond friendship with men, I've never been successful at it. Men are more than happy to talk to me, hang out with me, I'm blessed with that, but I'm not the kind of girl that guys put the moves on, if that makes sense. And I don't know why."

"Do you think you're going to ultimately have a family or you might not or you don't know?"

"I know that I would be fulfilled either way. I've never felt the drive to be a mother. I have friends who've known since we have been much younger that they wanted children, and that's great. But that was never my experience. I never thought, 'I can't wait to be a mother, I really want to be a mother.' If it happens, great, I'm totally open to it. If it doesn't happen, I think I'll be fine. But I do know, for example, that if I'm told I can't, then that I would have some difficulty with. But I'm open either way. If I don't have kids, then I'll be fine with it."

I respond, "Our work is very time-consuming and it's very emotionally draining. Does that enter into the equation for you?"

"Yes. I have thought about that a lot," Huma continues. "And I've come to the conclusion that I would need a fairly progressive partner, one that I'm — I don't know how — I don't think I'm all that likely to find within my culture, my ethnic demographic or whatever, because I've determined that we — because we don't work 9-to-5 days. We work around the clock sometimes. We wake up in the middle of the night. We have entire weeks where we're not home for dinner, and I'm just speaking from my limited experience as an associate attorney, not someone who's really in charge of the ship. I'll have weekends where I work the whole weekend through. I'll be up in the middle of the night sometimes on phone calls and this and that, and that's not conducive to going to ballet recitals or even making a date on a Friday night. Does that make sense?"

"It does," says Cyndy Short. "Anyone who has done intense work, like death penalty work, would understand." She smiles that dazzling smile. "I really had to learn how to be social. It didn't come naturally to me at all. So I had — because here's the other problem I had from a social standpoint: I couldn't bear to hurt anybody's feelings, so if anybody asked me out, I would go."

"Really? Oh, my goodness," I respond.

"Yeah. And there was this one fellow in college who, you know, had probably never been out with a girl, and he was, you know, the pocket pencil thing, and asked me to dance to 'Stairway to Heaven,' and that is the longest song in the whole world. And then he asked me to go to a basketball game or something, and I went. But that was kind of my attitude was I just didn't want to hurt anybody's feelings. Which is odd, I know, for someone who fights as hard as I do professionally." Not that odd I think to myself.

"Where did that come from?"

"I am not sure," Cyndy answers.

"Can you talk a bit about life/work balance for you? You have children?"

The Feminine Sixth: Women for the Defense

"I have three. I had my first child when I was in the public defender's office, and he was born in April of '92. The funny thing about being pregnant, as I'm sure you experienced, what was remarkable to me was how particularly the male judges acted as if you weren't pregnant. I'm not saying that they wouldn't mention it, but there was no special treatment for you as a pregnant person. I tried the case with Mitchell, I think. I was seven and a half months pregnant and I was trying a murder case. And the judge through all of that never once mentioned anything about my pregnancy. It was weird. No 'Do you need extra time?' No — it was just weird. It was almost like they were afraid to acknowledge it. I don't know if it was discriminatory or what they thought they were doing, but. . ."

"So the first one was in '92. Then I went to — let's see, he was born in '92, April, and I was in the Conflicts Office, and I took off the smallest amount of time that I could, like, six weeks, I think. It was the combination of having had the baby, trying cases, running the Conflicts Office, that I just wore out and made the decision to — it was after — no, it was before the — when I went to Trial Lawyers College, I was in a plaintiff's law firm. All right. So I'm getting my — so it was '93, I guess, I went to the plaintiff's law firm, which was a very big, well-respected law firm, and they came after me, which was very nice."

"Had you always planned to have children?"

"No. I came out of my family as the oldest child, saying, 'I'm done. I've babysat your children, I've taken care of these little ones. I'm done. I don't want a kid.' Even in college, I think I did not want kids. The funny thing is that of my siblings, I now have the most kids. So it wasn't until we got married that I started to feel like I wanted to have children, and, of course, he did. I didn't imagine having three; that wasn't my plan. Between the two of us, my husband is more maternal and he was also willing to be home while I was at work. And when I was trying cases, I could not have done it if Brian was not the personality that he is. Through particularly my public defender time, he did a lot of childcare, a lot of child rearing, I guess."

"It's interesting that you use the word 'maternal' to describe it. Why is that, why do you use the word 'maternal'?"

"Because he's — I am more stoic and closed off emotionally, I think — well, I know I am more than he is. He wears every single emotion on his sleeve. So sometimes there's this reverse: Emotionally I'm more made up like a man and he's more like a woman, but I've always been that. I've always thought of myself more emotionally in tune or like a man than a woman. I'm not saying — I didn't particularly love zero to five, to tell you truth, of child rearing. I thought that was really, really, really hard. I mean, I loved cuddling with the kids and all that stuff and spending a lot of time with the kids, but I was very passionate about what I did. I couldn't do it halfway, so I spent a lot of evenings and weekends working on cases while he was here. And particularly with Kyle, because Kyle was five before we had a second child. I could not have had children any closer together than that. That would have killed me, I think."

"Why do you say that?"

"I think the biggest challenge has been to have any kind of balance in my life because I only know how to do things one way, and it's kind of all in. Since I'm so consumed by it and there are periods of time where it's a seven-day-a-week kind of — like, last night, I was up at 1:00 a.m. and I thought of something, so I went ahead and texted it to whoever needed to do whatever it was I thought was so important. If Friday night comes up and I think, 'I'd really like to go to a movie,' who would I like to go to a movie with? The list is very small. I was thinking about this a lot a couple of years ago and I'm, like, why is it that I'm not invested in any real friendships? You know, I have friends who are baseball parents and I have friends who I work with, but I don't really have people outside of that. And then I started to realize that when you give all of your emotional energy to the clients — and I mentioned at lunch today that one of my clients calls me every week. Well, I represented him when he was 17, which was 22 years ago. At Christmas time and at birthdays, I make a special effort to remember people. And it started to occur to me, 'All of your emotional energy is being directed to the clients; you don't have that emotional stuff left to really invest in real people that aren't your clients.' So I think there's a loneliness to this, an isolation to it."

"I think that is something most of us, if not all of us have felt," I answer. "I have a very clear memory of my daughter at about three asking me 'Mommy who do you love more, me or your clients?'" I feel myself tear up a bit. "They sure know how to get to you don't they?" I can feel how hard this is hitting everyone.

Cynthia Roseberry walks over and puts her arm around my shoulder. "Let's take a little break."

CHAPTER SIX:
STILL STANDING

The last session had been pretty emotional. This was going to be more so I thought. Maybe not, but I was betting it would. "Well we are nearing the end of our day together," I say. The audience is tired I can tell, but they are still here. "Still with us?" I ask. I hear a few murmurs. "I can't hear you!" I say.

"Yes!" shouts someone from the audience. And then there were a few more yeses, and a few more, and then somehow we are all laughing.

"Well I am glad to hear it. We are now going to talk with the panelists about why they are staying with criminal defense, or have left it." I think for a moment. "There are moments of soul searching in any profession, I imagine. But in ours, there are many. We have been discussing all of the challenges of doing this work, as well as some of the joys, but I am going to ask our panelists to talk directly about the question of why they are still criminal defense lawyers, or why not."

I nod to the panel, and tell them that we are going to proceed in no particular order. So I turn to Cynthia Roseberry. "Do you ever consider leaving criminal defense? Do you ever get to a place where — I guess the question is: Why have you stayed, and have you ever considered leaving from doing this kind of work?"

"I've never considered leaving," she responds.

The Feminine Sixth: Women for the Defense

"Why do you think that is?"

"Of course, I've changed the way I'm in it, but I've never considered leaving it. You know, if I were still trying cases, I would say because I'm with my people. Criminal defense lawyers understand that there's racism in our nation, that there's sexism in our nation, and they understand those without having to chip away that shell and get to that with them, and that's a really comfortable place. Then outside of that in the other areas where I've worked, these issues are just too important for me to leave. I see them as my life's work. They're just — no. I take that back. One time I considered leaving trial work, and a lawyer said to me, 'If not you, then who?' And I realized that I accept it as a responsibility."

"Why were you thinking about leaving trial work?"

"It's difficult. I was doing a lot of federal work. The work is difficult work. The cases are proactively made. You don't win often. Clients go to prison for a long time, and it was just one case too many, one sad story too many, and I thought, I just can't do this. I need to do something else. I didn't know what else I was going to do, but I was just talking about leaving. And he said, 'If not you, then who?' And I realized, yeah, we need people in this work who care, not just people who are in this work to make money or for some title or people who will only represent people who have a lot of money to pay them. We need people who care about people who don't make a difference in the election because they have a felony conviction, right, and people who have been disrespected and mistreated all of their lives. They deserve one time that somebody respects their humanity. So in that way, it's a mission. I don't want to sound like –" Cynthia Roseberry trails off.

"Well, I was going to ask you about that," I step in. "You seem very cause-oriented or — I don't know if that's the right word — activist. I don't know what the right word is. But if you were going to describe your perspective on doing defense work, like, philosophically, or whatever word you want to use, how would you describe it?"

"Justice is love. When I die, I want my headstone, if there is one, to say, 'She loved.' To show someone justice, to seek justice for them, is to love them. It is to say you are worthy, you are as worthy as anybody else, so to love in that way when many times the love is unrequited, frankly. Clients have mental health issues or they have been mistreated and they don't trust you, they see you as part of the system. But some get it. Some get that you do it because you care. I remember a bond hearing when the only argument the prosecutor had left was to say, 'Well, you can't let him go on electronic monitoring; he doesn't even have a ride to get over to the probation office.' And I said, 'I'll take him,' and the courtroom stopped as if I had said, 'I'll chop his head off.' The probation officer said, 'You have to be careful about doing things like that.' I said, 'What are you talking about? This is a human being; I'll take him.' And on the ride over, the client, who had not been warm to me when I first met him, looked at me and he said, 'You know, I got you wrong and I owe you an apology. Thank you.' So yeah, justice is love."

"Crystal," I begin, "You have just retired after over twenty-five years as a public defender. So, imagine I am a much younger woman, and I'm thinking about being a criminal defense lawyer. What would you wisely advise me is good and bad, and how would you give me advice, one woman to another woman?"

The Feminine Sixth: Women for the Defense

Crystal tosses her head and takes a breath. "If you're the right kind of person. So woman aside, if you're the right kind of person. If you care, if your concern for getting — I think of it this way: If your concern for having people's stories told is bigger than you are, if you think it's important that people's stories are told, if you think it's important to listen to people and hear what they have to say, this is the greatest job going. This is a job that is going to be fulfilling and all-consuming and it's not going to feel like work, and you're going to be fulfilled intellectually and emotionally, and it's wonderful. You know, you have to take care of yourself, too. You have to make sure that you know what makes you happy to do and continue to do it in your personal life, whatever that is. Whatever that is, you've got to continue to do that. You've got to take care of yourself in this business like no other business because it's all-consuming. You literally could spend all of your time doing this work, and then you wouldn't be any good to anybody. You know, being a public defender, and we have a — we share a sense of humor like no other. The things we find funny, other people — you know, it's not meant for polite company."

The panelists are agreeing. We all know the bad jokes we often tell. "Yes," I say.

"But we witness and are the heart of some of the funniest things that can happen in a society. And we witness and are part of them in a way where we're not standing outside of it; we're actually part of it," Crystal continues.

"So what are you thinking you're going to do with retirement?"

"I think all public defenders need to be doing something with people, and here's the thing that I've kind of checked out: I love to read. I love to read anything. And I think it might be fun to tutor reading because I think that — my own belief is that it opens up so much for people, you know, not just school, but opens up different perspectives and different geographies and ways different people live, you know, all that. So I'm thinking about that as a possible kind of volunteer work." She looks at the audience a bit sheepishly. "There is still so much to do in the world," she says.

"Cyndy, do you find private criminal defense practice satisfying in the same way that you found being a public defender satisfying?"

"You know, I do," she says, and stops a moment.

"But?" I ask.

"I think I'm tired now, and I've got a lot on my plate right now. There have been times, Andrea, over the last, oh, decade, I would say, that I've really wanted a sabbatical, if I could just take a year off and kind of get recharged. And, bless my husband's heart, he's always, 'Oh, you wouldn't want to do that. You don't want to do that.' But he relies on the money that I bring in because I have an hourly practice and he has a contingency practice. So even though I work at the lowest end of the hourly rate scale, $125 an hour in federal court, $100 an hour in state court, and my staff, since they're independent contractors, they pay rent and all that sort of thing, and I supervise them. So we have an agreement in terms of that. But it's really challenging. And every year I will kind of think, well, I won't take as many cases, or I'm going to do something else. And then something walks in the door and I can't say no. And as soon as they walk in the door and you don't say no, you're tied in another two years minimally. So I don't know how long that will last. But I think the whole thing about balance and the challenge of being present when you're with your kids or with your family — and I jokingly

The Feminine Sixth: Women for the Defense

said today that I don't have any hobbies. I love movies, I love reading books. I do those things."

"You have been doing criminal defense for a long time," I observe.

"People often ask me, 'How did you stay in this this long?' And the answer is, 'Those successes.' And I think a lot of times the success, as we talked about, the way we have to measure success is different. I remember one client at a very contentious trial, one of my favorite cross-examinations of all time was of his wife. There was just too much joy surrounding that particular cross-examination for me. It went perfectly and she was so easy to prosecute, and you're feeling that adrenaline of having done that successfully and knowing you've connected with the jury. And afterward, in a quiet moment with the client, in a very sincere, tearful way, he looked at me and took my hands and he said, 'Thank you for giving me' — he said, 'my face back,' but what he meant was his identity. And that was the moment for me that really made all of the excruciatingly hard work leading up to that cross-examination worth it." She looks thoughtful. "It's those moments that keep you going."

I turn to Cynthia Stewart. "Once you started doing criminal defense, did you ever consider quitting, not doing it anymore, doing something else?" I ask.

"Not until recently. And I don't really want to quit now. It can be fun to practice law, and I wish we could find our way back to that. But I've got Laura Grace to finish getting through high school and then college." She shakes her head.

"Is that the only reason to keep going for you?"

"No, it is a big reason why I try not to get discouraged. Because I feel so tired and so exhausted, and I'm so — the fun part is not there."

"Could you describe what you mean by that?"

"I'm sure you've tried cases with co-counsel where sometimes there are amusing things that happen and you're enjoying it," she responds. "And sometimes that even extends to the judge enjoying it, not necessarily in front of the jury, and like doctors and other professionals, we have our own little sick senses of humor. There are judges now, the ones I practice in front of a lot, that are just terribly mean-spirited. They keep coming up with rules. They make everybody appear about five different times unless you've somehow pleaded out early. They are trying to completely control everything, including any deals, the behavior, everything."

"Do you regret any of the choices that you've made?"

"No," she responds quickly and firmly, but then her tone turns more contemplative. "There are parts of me that would have liked to quit or change somehow, but I think at this point I still can. I can pick that back up now. I've gotten them off to college; Laura Grace is pretty self-sufficient if I'm not there. I don't like leaving her for long periods of time; she misses her mama. And I think there are — we think of such a short period of time, so I — and I don't want to look — I do this anyway. I look back and think about the times Ann Gabriel wanted me to go to a movie with her. My girls love to do things with me. I regret the times I said no, but I think I said yes enough. In the broad race, I try. Either Saturday or Sunday, we'll go out. Just she and I will go to lunch and have a leisurely two-hour lunch somewhere we can sit. It's funny. As they came along, each one of my children loves to read

The Feminine Sixth: Women for the Defense

as much as I do, and sometimes they'd read at the table. So I told them, 'As long as we're all reading, it's okay.'"

I turn to Juanita. "Juanita, I am going to put you on the spot here — you are the only one of us who has left criminal defense (other than retiring). So can we talk about that a bit?"

"Sure," she says. "I am a trial lawyer and partner in a big firm — Fish Richardson — and I try patent cases. I gravitated that way in part I think because of my fascination with the forensic part of criminal cases, and for financial reasons. Patent law is constantly changing. So you may think you know the law, but wait until tomorrow because there's going to be something that's brand-new that's going to come down. And so it was just a really exciting idea, although a lot of people said, 'You're selling out.'"

"Do you feel that to some extent?"

"I do," she says.

"Would you talk about that a little?"

"Sure. I didn't get into being a criminal defense lawyer for the money. Obviously, I wouldn't have become a federal defender. For a very, very long time, until I basically stopped doing criminal defense, I still did appointed cases. There are plenty of lawyers who, once they start being successful in their practice, don't do appointed cases anymore. I did. And I would do cases for the NACDL Strike Force, which helps criminal defense lawyers whenever they are in trouble. So I didn't do it, I didn't get into it, for the money. And yet if I'm not doing it anymore, then I'm not doing my part. Now, I justified it, and my ex-husband Bart's helped me justify it by saying, 'Well, I made it possible for him to continue to be a public defender for the rest of his life because he didn't have to worry about supporting the kids and starting a college fund and putting them through school or anything like that.' So it was, like, maybe I made it possible then for someone to keep doing the good."

"I was still doing criminal defense when Cat Bennett (my dear friend and yours. She was the 'mother' of modern jury selection) passed away, and I think about what she would think of me now that I was not helping others. And I'm really not. I won, like, my first ten patent trials or something because no one's ever seen anybody like me in the patent world, right? I actually humanize things. And so the word was I couldn't lose. So finally I lost a trial that had already been tried once and lost, so I didn't feel that bad. And they hired me to try it and I was stuck with the police vehicle transcript and it was a deadly and uphill battle, but still I gave it my best shot. But when that adverse verdict was read in a patent case, I felt that same crushing feelings that the bottom fell out. I felt horrible. And I looked around. No one was crying. No one went into custody. I didn't have to think about sentencing. And in my head, I went, 'Oh, well, the judge will probably flip it. And if he doesn't, the federal circuit probably will. And if not, my company will pay them some money. Okay. I'm good.'"

"And I turned to my client, I'm, like, 'I'm sorry about that. Where would you like to have dinner?' And he looked at me, like, 'We just lost.' And I'm, 'Yeah, I know, but it's going to be fine. Don't worry about it.' Honestly, I put my heart into it, but —," she pauses.

"It doesn't feel the same?"

The Feminine Sixth: Women for the Defense

"It doesn't. It doesn't. And it shouldn't." Juanita nods emphatically.

"Huma," I say, "Can we talk about the same subject? Tell me what your thoughts are about being and staying a criminal defense lawyer."

Huma's impish grin is evident. "So I'm aware that I'm a bit of a cautionary tale because I'm aware that some mothers in my community do point at me to their daughters and they say, 'Well, pursue your schooling and do good and all that, but don't be like Huma; don't be like her because she's so focused on her career and she's still not married and she's getting older and it's probably not going to happen now,' which, to be honest, amuses me. I don't internalize that aspect of it because I'm very happy with what I do. I feel privileged every day."

"Do those comments affect you in any way?" I probe.

Huma laughs a little. "Actually I'm so spitefully happy because every social event I go to in our community, every family gathering, religious gathering, there are often young women there that are in junior high, they're in high school, they're in college, and they have heard about me. Some way or another, they've heard about me through their friends or through their aunts or whoever, they've heard about me, and they know what I do. And if they don't, they figure it out real quick. And that's all they want to talk about. So I tell them stories. I tell them some scary stories, I tell them some great stories, I tell them some really sad stories. Everywhere I go, occasionally I do — just a month or two ago I did a career fair at my mom's school, and whenever I go to a dinner party or a holiday or whatever, so many girls come up to me and

they're, like, 'We want to be criminal defense attorneys.'"
She pauses.

"And they seem to understand that being a criminal defense attorney is so much more demanding than just sitting at a desk for a few hours a day and pushing through your paperwork and then going home to your domestic life. It's really demanding and it's unpredictable, and they seem to know that. So it's so pleasing to me to see them have that enthusiasm while their mothers exhibit a bit of trepidation about it, because we need more female attorneys, we need more people of color who are attorneys, and we can benefit from more Muslim female attorneys. It's so weird to me to think that it's because of me, and I don't think it is. I think they see it on TV and all that, but I think I make it real; I think I make it a bit more real for them, because when they see me, they see themselves. They say, 'She comes from our background, she has parents just like ours, she went to an Islamic school like we did, she went to a public college like we did, and she's doing this and she seems to not be making a total hash of it.'"

There is laughter, a warm laughter in the audience and among the panel.

"So that's what they're attracted to and that's what they want to do, and they're seeing that they have that option, that even if their parents don't necessarily agree with it, they have that option, they can do it. So that's what I am really very grateful for, that I have the chance to do that."

"Because they're not thinking about it in terms of 'If I'm a criminal defense attorney, then I'm going to end up married to a wealthy doctor, because that will be an attractive thing.' They're thinking, 'I want to do criminal defense because it's interesting, because it's challenging, because it's going to be intellectually stimulating, because Huma's doing it and it looks like she's having so much fun, and now I can imagine myself doing it.' And it's not related to anything else; it's just for the passion of it, which I think is really important, because there seem to be a lot of attorneys that don't have that passion, and that doesn't seem to end well for a lot of people," Huma continues.

"There's a fulfillment that's very hard to describe to someone who hasn't done it of knowing you have so much against you, but you still managed to eke out a little victory that saved someone a little bit of pain or a little bit of fear or something."

"Christine," I turn to Christine Start. "You're young, you've been doing this for six years, more or less?"

"Yeah. I got my bar card in December 2010."

"Have you ever thought you're going to leave, that you're going to leave criminal defense work or leave being a public defender?"

"I have. I got certified as a coach. Not that I want to be a coach full-time, but I really like that aspect — it's not a therapist, it's not a counselor, but it's someone that helps you get from where you are to where you want to be."

"A life coach kind of thing?" Ah California, I think.

She nods. "Kind of like that, but then they use them a lot in corporations, especially like executive and leadership and things like that. It's really fun, because I would like to coach my clients, and sometimes I do once in a while. The answer is really within the person. It's not me telling them what to do.

Something sticks when you yourself come up with what you should be doing, right? It's really cool. So I really enjoyed that. So I was, well, let me just take this course because I can do it on the side, and let me get certified because it's just really interesting and I like it." She furrows her brow, looking for how to explain it.

"You see, there's a big difference between helping someone that really, really needs your help because they can't do it without you, which is what I do for a living, and helping someone that is in a place in their life where they can be helped and then have the resources and ability to actually do something about it, right? Different circumstances. It gets really tiring being a public defender in that sense because especially now that I'm a felony attorney and I have a lot of the parole cases, I see, like, the same clients all the time. You get tired of seeing the same clients do the same things. And then it's just part of this wheel where you want to make a difference, but for these clients or this client in particular, you can't change them. You just have to help mitigate, right, like get them the least time as possible and not be super emotionally attached because it's just going to drain you because they'll probably be back. So I asked myself, do I want to do this forever? What if it comes down to my family or the work?

"So I started just to explore what else interested me, and coaching was really interesting, I'm still doing that. But now I'm in this weird path now, like, right now. Like, your letter asking me to participate in this couldn't have come at a better time for me because I know that my passion lies in doing criminal defense work, criminal law work, or prison work for the indigent community. I notice that I just enjoy helping people and connecting with people that most of society doesn't want to help or connect with. And there's

The Feminine Sixth: Women for the Defense

something really powerful about that for me I'm not done yet, but this whole idea of 'I know that my life's passion, or whatever this calling is that I'm having right now, is connected to me wanting to show others the humanity of these people that are marginalized, that they're human, too' That's it. Whether that be as a public defender, whether that be like opening up my own nonprofit and going into different prisons and visiting people and hearing their stories, I am committed to trying to make a difference." She grins. "As corny as that sounds."

"Lisa, could you tell a story where you felt, 'I'm who I should be, doing what I should be doing,' during a trial, talking to a client, whatever, it doesn't matter?"

"It wouldn't be during a trial. It's interesting. I don't value myself on my victories, and I've had a lot. I mean, I've been super lucky in my life, I think. I've won way more cases than I've lost, and I've tried a ton. I've tried over 150 jury trials, but that's not the greatest point. And I think talking to my clients, I think my greatest — knowing this is what I do, is the client, the rare client for me, for whatever reason, that comes back and tells you of their personal success because you saved their life. Yeah. I don't think about these things. I hear a lot of defense lawyers saying, 'God, it never feels like we're making any inroads and we're just a cog in the wheel, and we're not really doing anything great. We're just part of the system.' And I never feel that way because there are those individual stories where you really have made a difference, not in the courtroom, but giving people a second chance. I got second chances, and everybody, I don't care what you've done in your worst moment, deserves a second chance. I think that's what drives me is the second chances."

"What would you say to a young woman who was considering criminal defense work?"

"It's the best job you can have as a woman if you are a believer, if this is your passion. It's the best job. I'm at the point after 30 years, I think, you've got to do something else. You've got to do other things in your life. I look at you and I look at some of the other women friends of mine, and at times they've changed it up in some way. I mean, they're still connected to this, but they've changed it up. And I think of myself, particularly when you do these long trials, Andrea, I'm much more beat up physically than I was as a young lawyer. And I remember hearing it's a young person's game, 'A young man's game,' is what they told us, not a young woman's game. You're beat up. And then I think, oh, in my mind, like I said earlier, I can't remember what I did yesterday, but I can remember what I did 50 years ago, almost, but I can't remember what I did yesterday. And I think on these big cases where I do volumes of discovery, these white-collar cases. Am I going to remember, you know? You do. So none of that has — but it's the best job in the world in terms of rewarding. I wake up and look at myself in the mirror and go, 'Okay, you look a little older, but, damn, you have such a great life and job,' right? I can't imagine that every job is that fulfilling. Maybe being a doctor that would be the only other job I would have been is a doctor, I think, or a priest."

"That is interesting," I respond. "Do you think you'll retire, that you'll stop? Not that you're retirement age yet, but you can see where you will be at some point."

"If I'd only met a rich man in my life, then you have the luxury of working all your life or not, right?" She sighs dramatically and ironically. "I don't plan on retiring. Here are the things I think of at this point in my life, at 56: I see how much it takes

The Feminine Sixth: Women for the Defense

out of me physically, because I want to remain effective, so it goes to, 'Am I still tough and effective?' And so far, so good, but I don't feel the same. As I've gotten older, I live with my cases way more than I did when I was young."

"Talk to us a bit more about that."

"Yeah. It's interesting. Look, when we were public defenders, you had heartbreaking cases, and I cared about my cases. I don't think I would ever be characterized as a hand holder, so there are a lot of my colleagues and a lot of my female colleagues that did that kind of mothering thing, always going out to see the client, bringing the family stuff, blah-blah-blah. I never was like that. I was like, I care about you, and I'm going to fight like hell for you. I became very close to some of my clients, but I was never a hand holder, but I cared about them. But I didn't lose sleep. I wake up in the morning a lot thinking about my clients and I didn't do that when I was young. And I don't think that's menopause. I don't know if it's motherhood, I don't know if I get the consequences and the collateral consequences so much more and I see so much more and I'm out maybe on the policy thing and I've seen — I don't really know, Andrea, but I lose sleep, and I don't know how long you can do that. I don't know how long you can just be in this angst a lot, and I'm angry. But you know what, Andrea? At the end of the day, I mean, I don't have any envy directed toward a man and go, 'Oh, I wish I could be like him,' or 'I wish I could look like that.' I love being the different one in the courtroom. Don't you? I love it. I really do. I mean, you don't really have a choice, I guess — well, I guess you do have a choice. But I am where I want to be, where I am needed, and doing what I should be doing."

"Amanda, what about you?" I ask. "Have you ever thought that you might leave criminal defense at some point?"

Nodding, Amanda says she has.

"Can you tell us about that a little bit?

"I have thought — there's times when I've thought, this is not sustainable, I can't do this forever, I can't care this much forever. There are times when I've thought that this is not the most effective way. The problems are bigger than the ones I'm dealing with standing in the courtroom, you know? Being there is kind of like putting a Band-Aid on a bullet hole. What am I really doing? I don't think that time is anytime soon. I also think that longevity-wise, I'll be better off if I can combine being in courtrooms with advocating for policy change. In the context of the clemency cases I have been working on, I've been really re-energized by talking about sentencing reform and pushing sentencing reform because there's that bill pending in Congress right now, and I think knowing that there's not just these individuals, but that I'm also able to give my piece about what could help on a broader scale. That gives me energy and makes me feel a little more hope. I feel revitalized by that."

"Both as a supervisor and as a former public defender, a big problem was burn out. Do you ever worry about burning out yourself?" I ask.

"Yes, I do. I think working at the Cook County Public Defender's office during that summer before my last year of law school was very eye-opening about burnout. Because the thing about burnout is not because people stop caring; that's not it at all. I think I've realized, and I think actually being in social work school has helped me name what's going on, like vicarious trauma is real. What's happening to our clients is very traumatic, and we are by their side going through the system if we really care. I think it would be much easier and burnout would be not be an issue if you don't care a whole lot." She stops, thinking.

"It appears to me you have some final thoughts or questions or things you think ought to be in this conversation," I observe. She smiles in acknowledgment.

"I think this conversation is so important, and I am so excited that you're facilitating this. And in whatever form — this book that comes from our conversation, I think, is great. I hope it starts with the book. I hope people make connections, I hope women make connections with each other so that we can continue to support each other. I think we all want to see a more just U.S.A., and to do that, we have to link arms with each other. We have to." The audience starts applauding. They are inspired, and frankly so am I. "Well," I say, "That about wraps it up."

"Oh no it doesn't," interrupts Cynthia Roseberry. "We all want to hear what keeps you going. Don't we?" She looks out at the audience. "Don't we?!" She repeats herself and there is an enthusiastic "yes" that comes from the audience and the panel.

I realize I really should say something, and so I nod. "Let me leave you with a story then," I say. "It's about a case I lost. Okay?"

"So about the case that I lost. It was a murder case, and the evidence against my client Darryl was all circumstantial. But there was a *lot* of it." I take a breath. "You know what I mean, right?" I look at my nodding colleagues. "I mean there was this first piece of circumstantial evidence, and I could do something about that, and then there was this second bit of circumstantial evidence, and I could take that apart, and then, well a third, a fourth...at a certain point it just tipped. They were going to convict." I pause a moment. "And they did, they were out deliberating for a few hours, but they convicted him. So the judge thanks them for their service and excuses them from the courtroom. We set a date for post-trial motions and sentencing, and the sheriffs were walking Darryl back to the lock up when he stopped and said to the judge 'Judge, can I say something?' Well this isn't a good moment. The judge tries to head it off by telling my client that he should let his lawyer — me — speak for him. Darryl says 'But what I want to talk about is my lawyer.'"

I look out at the audience. "For those of you who might not know, this isn't a good moment. It means that the defendant is likely going to complain about the job you did in an effort to establish that you were ineffective. Which is fair game, but unlikely to endear him to the judge who is going to pick from 'a really long time' sentence on up to a 'never getting out' sentence. As an aside, any criminal defense lawyer will tell you that when you see a client coming out of the lock up with a big cross around his neck, a file and a bible you know *nothing good* is going to happen that day!" I laugh and see not only the panel laughing with me, but the audience too.

"So anyway, the judge agrees reluctantly. 'Is that lady writing this down?' Darryl asks, pointing at the court reporter. The judge sighs and says 'yes.' 'Good,' he says, 'Cause I want her to write down that I thank Miss Lyon.'" I turn to the panel. "Can you believe it? He just lost and is going away for a long time at best, and he is *thanking* me?!" I take a breath. I am tearing up a bit. "So he continues on, and says 'I didn't give her much to work with, but no one has ever fought for me

The Feminine Sixth: Women for the Defense

before. So you write it down,' he says again, and points to the court reporter. 'I want it wrote down that I thank her.'"

Crystal says "that's what it is about, isn't it?" I nod.

The room stands applauding, many with tears like mine in their eyes. I walk back to the panel, and they surround me, hugging me, and we all walk off the stage together.♀

The Feminine Sixth: Women for the Defense

NOTES

The Feminine Sixth: Women for the Defense

The Feminine Sixth: Women for the Defense